HIDDE
DERBYSHIRE

Richard Stone

Other Derbyshire titles available from Countryside Books include:

TALES OF OLD DERBYSHIRE
Elizabeth Eisenberg

DERBYSHIRE: A PORTRAIT IN COLOUR
Bill Meadows and William Amos

DERBYSHIRE GHOSTS AND LEGENDS
David Bell

EY UP MI DUCK
Richard Scollins & John Titford

PUB STROLLS IN DERBYSHIRE
Charles Wildgoose

WATERSIDE WALKS IN DERBYSHIRE
Charles Wildgoose

HIDDEN
DERBYSHIRE

Richard Stone

COUNTRYSIDE BOOKS
NEWBURY, BERKSHIRE

COUNTRYSIDE BOOKS
3 Catherine Road
Newbury, Berkshire

To view our complete range of books,
please visit us at
www.countrysidebooks.co.uk

ISBN 1 85306 715 6

Illustrations and map by Helen Stone

The front cover picture taken by Bill Meadows
shows Peveril Castle, Castleton,
from above Cave Dale.

The back cover picture taken by the author
shows one of the ornate street lamps
in the Crescent, Buxton.

Produced through MRM Associates Ltd., Reading
Printed by J. W. Arrowsmith Ltd., Bristol

INTRODUCTION

Hidden Derbyshire, now there's a challenge. The area covered by the Peak District National Park is one of the most familiar and best loved in all the country — and rightly so. There are innumerable reference books and guides to the county. TV documentaries take millions of viewers 'behind the scenes' at stately homes such as fabulous Chatsworth House. But despite Derbyshire's popularity what do we still miss? What goes unnoticed? What do we take for granted? What is worth the effort of going the extra mile to seek out? Generations of my family have lived in Derbyshire and I have rarely strayed beyond walking distance of its borders. Writing this book has given me the opportunity to revisit and reflect upon the diverse corners of this singularly interesting county.

What became increasingly clear to me as I began to put my thoughts in order is the importance of understanding our surroundings in context. Conservation is now high on the national agenda but change is inevitable and difficult decisions — about land use, housing, transport — still have to be faced. History and nature have much to teach us about our place in the scheme of things and the value of caring sensitively for our surroundings. So this book aims not just to be simply about features in isolation but to build a bigger picture from the detail of the Derbyshire countryside and the factors that have shaped it: wildlife; people and how they lived, worked and travelled; their folklore and customs; geology; and industry.

My thanks to all who tune in to broadcasts on BBC Radio Derby or read articles in the *Burton Mail*, especially those who take the time to share their knowledge and enthusiasm for local history and the countryside. And to all who put up with listening to me in the 'snug' at the Anorak and Whistle: You can wake up now — but I'll be asking questions later!

Richard Stone

HIDDEN
DERBYSHIRE

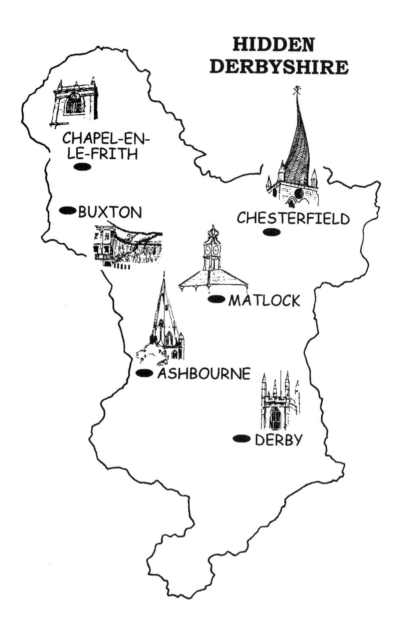

CHAPEL-EN-
LE-FRITH

BUXTON

CHESTERFIELD

MATLOCK

ASHBOURNE

DERBY

ALDERWASLEY

—— Before it became a school, the Georgian hall at Alderwasley was home to the Hurt family, who built an extensive industrial empire in the 18th and 19th centuries based on iron founding. Alderwasley Park has fine views over the Derwent Valley to Crich Chase. High open grassland cropped close by sheep and pitted with rocky outcrops falls gradually away to the point where the woods of Shining Cliff begin a more marked descent into the valley casting a deep shadow over the A6 below. Beside a path, near a stand of oak and sweet chestnut, is an old yew tree, its branches broken by the weight of years to shortened stumps.

In the 18th century, when the yew was in its prime, this was the site of a charcoal burner's camp. For several months each year the Kenyon family, husband, wife and eventually eight children, set up home beneath the thick, leafy canopy. Successive Kenyon babies are said to have enjoyed a makeshift crib hollowed out of one of the lower yew branches, inspiring the nursery rhyme *Rock-a-bye baby*.

Charcoal kilns have to be constantly attended to ensure that they burn at the correct rate so living on the job was a necessity. To construct a kiln, lengths of wood called cords are built up from the ground in a triangular shape to make a flue. Around this, logs cut to a similar size are stacked vertically, gradually building the circle of poles outwards before laying more lengths to roof the construction. The kiln is finished with a thatch of turf or bracken and sealed with earth before being lit by dropping a glowing ember into the central flue. The secret of the charcoal burners' craft was to control the burning by restricting the flow of air and they were constantly repairing holes or creating vents as the kiln smouldered. When the charcoal was judged to be ready water was used to extinguish the fire, the complete process taking two to three days depending on the size of the kiln. As one kiln burned others were constructed and fired to maintain a continuous process.

Charcoal delivers high temperatures, twice the heat delivered by the same amount of wood or coal, and was much in demand for iron smelting. Wood for the kiln needed to be a uniform length and thickness and this was achieved by coppicing. This was an efficient form of woodland management using the regenerative power of many trees to grow new branches if cut back to a 'stool' just above the ground. It took around 2,000 acres of woodland to produce enough charcoal to keep an average sized blast furnace in business. By working Shining Cliff in sections and rotating the coppicing over a 20 year cycle, charcoal burning could take place here for perhaps six months every year with a guaranteed supply of suitable material. Shining Cliff Wood was replanted early in the 20th century and bears little resemblance today to the managed woodland that preceded it.

Charcoal burners traditionally constructed shelters for themselves and their families using turf and sacking over a frame of poles or a suitable horizontal tree branch and were a feature of the woodland scene within living memory. Gradually demand diminished and now it is mainly used to fire up home barbecues. Cooking in the garden may seem like the outdoor life but try to imagine living and sleeping beneath the old yew tree in Alderwasley Park for a few months every year. And by the way, did I mention Shining Cliff Wood is supposed to be haunted?

ALPORT

—— The name of this pretty village 3 miles south of Bakewell means 'Old Town' or 'Old Market Place'. There has been an important river crossing here, where the Lathkill and Bradford meet, for many centuries. A wide and unpredictable ford was replaced with a bridge for the first time in 1718. A second road bridge followed in 1793. Hard to believe this picturesque place was once a hive of industry. Like many Peakland villages it grew rich on the profits of lead mining but it also had its textile and paper-pulping mills. If you are eagle-eyed, and know where to look, the evidence remains. From the road, a quarter of a mile north of the village, the ruins of two large lead-smelting reverberatory furnaces lie across the river, well concealed in undergrowth. The site is private but the remains can just be made out nestling into the hillside on the opposite bank. This was one of the main local works in the 19th century. Although condensing flues ran up to a chimney high on the hillside the site seems much too close to the village for comfort given the toxic nature of lead vapour. Now that the business is no more it is easy to forget such activity was ever carried out in such a tranquil and picturesque spot.

ANCHOR CHURCH

A footpath to the west of tiny Ingleby leads along a slight scarp with fine views over the Trent Valley before dropping to the riverside. After half a mile, where the river loops away to the north, the path continues beside a small oxbow known as 'Black Pool'. According to local legend, the invading Danish warriors moored their dragon-prowed longboats here in the winter of AD 873. They too would most likely have gazed upon Anchor church, carved deep into the solid rock, its open windows and doorways gaping through the curvature of the outer surface like the features on some giant Hallowe'en pumpkin. Inside, the main chamber has two supporting pillars and a surround of arched semicircular niches. The Anchorite's Larder, a smaller cave, lies just a little further along the path.

An anchorite, or hermit, may have made this their retreat in the early days of Christianity. Medieval sources mention a 7th century recluse, St Hardulph, living in a cave in the vicinity. The earliest reliable evidence of an inhabitant comes from the parish records of Repton. These refer to 'Ye foole at Anchor church' in 1658.

A century later, following the Georgian fashion for eccentric venues in which the gentry could entertain and amuse guests, the local squire from Foremark had doors and windows fitted and converted the main chamber into a dining room. Those Georgian additions have long since vanished to leave the bare rock much as it must have been centuries before. Silent, secluded and atmospheric, staring broodily northwards over the flat river plain.

ASHBOURNE

This stylish market town and 'Gateway to the Peak' has its share of tea-rooms and antique shops but still bustles with everyday life. North of the medieval street pattern that follows the valley bottom contour of Henmore Brook, the town climbs steeply onto the limestone plateau of the White Peak.

A short stroll along St John Street and Church Street as far as the parish church, St Oswald's, takes in more than five centuries of fashionable building. The oldest property is the Gingerbread Shop. A mock Tudor mask hid a jettied upper storey for years before its original design was discovered. Oversailing jetties were a practical innovation popular in timber-framed houses until the middle of the 15th century. Unlike the case with modern building practice, early joists were cut in rectangular section and laid broad side down like thick planks. The result

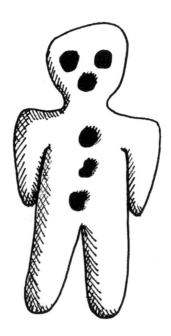

A gingerbread man from Ashbourne.

was floors that were unnervingly springy. Projecting the joists to form an overhang above the ground floor cured the bounce and provided a bonus in useful extra space upstairs. As a design feature, the jetty was replaced in Jacobean times in favour of the stability achieved by laying joists on their narrow edge.

Many of the houses — for example, the Old Grammar School, the Mansion, Pegg's Almshouses — have explanatory plaques. But the real character of Ashbourne lies in the detail. Narrow alleys, many spilling out onto the triangular cobbled market place, thread between Jacobean and Georgian frontages, giving access to more modest properties set discreetly behind. Look closely at the Black's Head on the unusual 'gallows' sign of the Green Man and Black's Head Royal Hotel that spans St John Street. It has a different expression on each side. And though graceful St Oswald's catches the eye, notice how the pyramid shaped stones that cap the gatepost pillars of its elaborate wrought iron gates rest on macabre sculpted skulls.

Bottled Ashbourne water is popular today in shops, bars and restaurants but it was 1896 before its inhabitants enjoyed a fresh water supply. Concerned about public health, Captain Holland, of Ashbourne Hall, had campaigned vigorously for the local wells to be replaced. In Belle View Road, parallel to Church Street behind the Old Grammar School, a solitary cast iron street pump remains as a testament to his efforts.

ASHFORD-IN-THE-WATER

The A6 Bakewell to Buxton road follows a line south of the river Wye, crossing the river upstream of Ashford and thereby avoiding the picturesque jumble of houses on the northern bank. Ashford would be a top contender in any most beautiful village in Derbyshire competition. Sheepwash Bridge, a narrow three-arched packhorse crossing and the oldest of the village bridges, is a popular and much photographed spot. At one end the stone parapet extends and curls around to form an enclosure. Flocks of sheep from the surrounding hills were once driven down to holding pens on the south bank in early summer to be spruced up before shearing. Farmers were charged for the

Sheepwash Bridge at Ashford-in-the-Water

privilege of dunking their sheep providing a 'nice little earner' for the Ashford Parish Council.

The village's main money-spinner from the late 18th century and throughout the Victorian era was a local speciality, Black Marble. This highly polished variety of dark hued limestone was cut from two local quarries at Rookery Plantation, beside the A6 north of the village, and Arrock Quarry in nearby Kirk Dale. A plaque on the south wall of Holy Trinity church commemorates Henry Watson, the founder of the industry.

At the church, do not miss four faded paper garlands in the north aisle. These are maiden's garlands, sometimes known as 'virgin's crants' or 'crowns', survivors of a touching Peak funeral custom marking the sad passing of girls who died before their wedding day.

Downstream of the village is Flewitt's corn mill, standing on an island in the river Wye created by the mill leats. In the 1970s, when a water turbine replaced two undershot waterwheels, this was one of the last water-powered mills still operating as a commercial enterprise. The current building is 18th century but Ashford is an ancient village and it is likely there has been a mill on this spot since the days when it was a Saxon royal estate.

ASHOVER

—— Fancy a stroll on deck? Since Derbyshire has all the coastline of Switzerland you know it is a trick question but nevertheless an apt way of introducing Great Eastern plantation. This small wood looks over the Amber Valley from Overton Hall to where the rocky ridge of 'The Fabrick' (the name is said to derive from land given for rebuilding and repairs to the fabric of local churches) rises to almost 1,000 feet.

There has been an estate at Overton since at least the early Middle Ages. The current hall, now a residential home for the elderly, was built, according to its datestone, in 1702. One of its former owners, Sir Joseph Banks, sailed around the globe with Captain James Cook in the *Endeavour*. The nautical influence clearly stayed in the air because less than a century after Cook's epic voyage, the launching of Isambard Kingdom Brunel's *Great Eastern* steamship, in 1858, inspired this patch of woodland that can be walked through following a footpath from Back Lane along the escarpment to Fallgate.

The boundary of the plantation is laid out to match the length and beam of the ship. It shows just what a mighty vessel the *Great Eastern* was and why she captured the public's imagination. Brunel's brief was to build a ship that could carry 12 months' worth of exports to India in a single cargo and to return without refuelling. Economy was achieved by using two paddle wheels and a propeller supplemented by a huge area of canvas on four masts. The *Great Eastern* remained the largest ship afloat for 40 years. All aboard?

AULT HUCKNALL

—— Westminster Abbey is the obvious place to look for memorials to pre-eminent Englishmen, not one of the smallest churches in Derbyshire. Yet in the modest church of St John the Baptist in this attractive village is buried the celebrated 17th century philosopher and writer Thomas Hobbes.

Hobbes met the most famous thinkers of his day, including Galileo and Descartes, and is most famous for *Leviathan*, a political treatise on sovereignty. Although born in Wiltshire and much travelled he spent most of his life employed as tutor to the Devonshire family at Chatsworth House and Hardwick Hall. The Derbyshire countryside that Hobbes loved was, as much as anywhere, his home and so it is perhaps appropriate that his final resting place is here overlooking Hardwick Hall Country Park.

BAKEWELL

The 'Gateway to the Peak' is a handsome town. A mix of stone properties dating back to Tudor times and tasteful modern additions that blend harmoniously along the folds of the meandering river Wye. It is also a visitor magnet. The town centre, around the Rutland Arms, a Georgian coaching inn renamed from the White Lion in 1805 in honour of the Duke at nearby Haddon Hall, and the Old Pudding Shop, is frequently overrun. Bakewell Pudding, one of the world's great bloomers, was the result of a recipe error by an assistant cook in the White Lion kitchens who mistakenly lined a pastry case with jam before adding cake mixture.

Leave the crowds to rub shoulders in the Market Square and take a stroll out of town along Buxton Road. On the right hand side you will soon pass the site of Victoria Mill, now a business centre. Corn was milled here until the 1940s. Now the old waterwheel rusts quietly in the yard outside. From here, the road is accompanied by the former millstream. A short distance beyond is Holme Bridge. This fine bridge, restored in 1664, was used by the packhorse trains to avoid paying a toll in the town centre. With characteristically low parapets it is just wide enough to allow horses with full panniers to cross in single file. Trains of 20 or more animals, carrying balanced loads of perhaps 2½ hundredweight on wooden frames, regularly travelled the same set routes that had been used for centuries. This made the men who worked on the packhorse trains a welcome source of news and gossip in isolated communities.

Just upstream of Holme Bridge are the weir and a sluice gate where water was diverted into a trench, or leat, to drive the mill

Bakewell's Holme Bridge.

wheel. On a triangle of land formed between the millstream and the course of the river is a small stone-walled enclosure. Sheep were penned here as they waited to be washed in the leat before shearing.

Across the bridge, behind a converted farm building that has signs of a dovecote incorporated below the roof gable, is Jacobean Holme Hall, with a battlemented tower and walled garden visible from the road. A little further upstream is the site of Lumford Cotton Mill beyond the row of workers' cottages built by Richard Arkwright in 1778.

Brave the bustle back in Bakewell, because All Saints' church is a 'must see'. Standing in an elevated position the octagonal spire is clearly visible from most of the town. It has some excellent Saxon carvings in the south porch and a Saxon cross 8 feet high. Look closely at the cross. It may be as old as the 8th century and reflects, or possibly reconciles, the religious conflicts of that time. On one side it depicts Christian scenes including the crucifixion, on the other can be made out Yggdrasil, the world tree, and Ratakosk, a squirrel symbolising life, from Norse mythology. What most visitors miss are the unusual carvings on some of the coffin lids in the churchyard. These show the occupation, for example an axe for a woodman, of the person at rest beneath.

BALLIDON

A large quarry eating into the limestone edge behind Ballidon overshadows a thin scatter of old farm buildings and some more recent cottages. The village has shrunk and moved since the foundations for tiny All Saints' chapel were first dug. Both the Black Death and the hunger of monastic landowners for sheep pasture played a part in the demise of the early settlement and now the chapel stands alone in fields.

Ballidon is a textbook example of the signs associated with a deserted medieval village. An isolated church where footpaths meet surrounded by the earthworks of house platforms and medieval ridge and furrow ploughing patterns trapping the shadows in the nearby fields. Deserted medieval villages were first recognised as recently as the 1940s. Since then, thousands have been identified and doubtless many more await discovery.

Beyond the quarry entrance, a track leads northwards towards remote Roystone Grange. In this hidden valley, largely ignored by the many walkers passing close by on the High Peak Trail, two thousand years of farming and occupation have been extensively studied and interpreted by a team from Sheffield University. Large stones known as 'orthostats' form the base of some of the drystone walling and reveal their Roman period origins. Terraces and field banks from this early period are visible on the west-facing slope south of the Grange while north of the modern farm, behind an old dairy, is the site of a Roman villa. Granges were monastic farms and, in the Middle Ages, Roystone was run by Cistercian lay brothers on behalf of their mother house at Garendon in Leicestershire. The fabric of the medieval farm was probably recycled into the buildings that stand today.

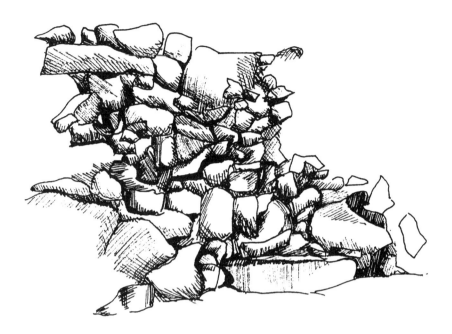

An orthostat wall at Ballidon.

A recommended circular walk exploring the valley and its wealth of industrial and rural archaeology begins at a car park on the High Peak Trail, half a mile south of Pikehall. The route is waymarked by yellow arrows marked with the letter 'R' and takes about four hours.

BARLBOROUGH

This little visited corner of the county is close to the boundaries of Yorkshire and Nottinghamshire. The M1 motorway slices between Barlborough and its close neighbour Spinkhill — a visible sign that could perhaps be seen as a metaphor symbolising the differences between two families that were once the most powerful and influential in the area. The Protestant Rodes and the Roman Catholic Poles represent two sides of a historical divide and there is a twist to the tale.

The former properties of both families are less than 2 miles apart. Both can be seen from footpaths. Barlborough Hall in landscaped parkland is the most impressive. Built by Francis de Rodes, a leading judge, in 1584, it is an unusual square Tudor mansion with octagonal turrets at each corner. Francis de Rodes is also responsible for Barlborough Old Hall that stands in the village. His descendants built Barlborough School while the Pole family donated the 18th century almshouses.

At a time when being a practising Roman Catholic was fraught with danger (see the entries for Derby and Padley) the Poles, of Spinkhill Hall and Park Hall (now a hotel), managed to observe their faith and avoid the enthusiastic priest-hunters. But recusant families still paid a cost in social exclusion and occasional fines. In an interesting turn of fate, Barlborough Hall now serves as a preparatory school for Mount St Mary's Roman Catholic College that is based at Spinkhill Hall.

BARROW UPON TRENT

Robert de Bakepuze gave St Wilfrid's church at Barrow to the Knights of St John of Jerusalem in 1197, shortly after the 3rd Crusade. With the church came income from tithes and land. The Knights Hospitallers, as they were familiarly known (see Yeaveley entry), stayed here until 1540, when fallout from the Reformation led to changes. In later years the centre at Barrow had become closely connected to the preceptory at Stydd Hall, near Yeaveley. While historical records show the Hospitallers had a base at Barrow they do not reveal where it was located.

Arleston Hall, now the privately owned Arleston House Farm, is the most likely site. This two-storey building is in a fairly isolated spot over a mile north-west of the village. The best approach, offering a good but respectfully discreet view, is along the towpath of the Trent and Mersey Canal. A combination of brick and some half-timbered box framing represent different ages of development in the house's history. Buttressed stone foundations are older and could easily be of an appropriate, early medieval date. Outside the house an intriguing assortment of large dressed stone blocks, including one in a cruciform shape, decorate the grass verge but a conclusive link to connect the house with the Hospitallers has proved elusive. An alternative site, that of Barrow's old hall in the village centre which burned down in 1957, is now a modern residential development and unlikely to yield any clues.

Back in the village do not miss a charming row of neat red-brick cottages, built in the 18th century from the proceeds of a parish levy.

BASLOW

'Stands the church clock at C to A? And is there honey still for tea?' Something wrong here but this is Baslow not Grantchester. St Anne's church clock reads VICTORIA 1897 in place of the usual numerals, a novel celebration of the Queen's Diamond Jubilee. Inside, the church still has its dog whip. A reminder of a time when working dogs accompanied their masters on the Sunday trek from outlying areas. The dog-whipper was a church appointee usually paid a few pence to keep order during services.

The oldest part of the village, Bridge End, is next to the church. The three-arched stone bridge crossing the river Derwent here dates from around 1600 when it replaced an earlier wooden structure. Do not miss the diminutive watch house built into the parapet. A tollhouse stood across the road until a century ago but the watch house pre-dates this and was

St Anne's church clock at Baslow.

St Anne's church, Baslow still has its dog whip.

manned to ensure the bridge was not subjected to too much
heavy traffic. Millstones in particular were a problem and a
charge was introduced in 1500 in response to concern about the
wear and tear caused by their transport across the bridge.
Standard practice for moving millstones was to fit them in pairs
like wheels at either end of a wooden axle so that they could be
rolled. The main road now crosses a little further downstream
but the old bridge once carried significant traffic through
Baslow. Follow Bar Road, a steep track leading east from Over
End, and you will find the clues that this was once a regular
packhorse trail. By a sharp bend is a water trough. Higher up
still, traces of paving slabs and where the path begins to cross
the moorland of Eaglestone Flat with its monument to the Duke
of Wellington (Nelson is similarly commemorated on these
heights) there is a guidestone. The weather-etched Eagle Stone
outcrop is nearby. In a kind of high altitude stag party ritual
the young men of Baslow were supposed to prove their mettle
by climbing this crag before their wedding day.

BEELEY

Over 30 Bronze Age barrows and cairns are scattered on bleak and windswept Beeley Moor. It rises to over 1,200 feet and the steep lower slopes are thickly wooded. Beeley Brook rises on the moor to dance and cascade down a series of waterfalls before joining the waters of the river Derwent.

Beeley sits on the doorstep of Chatsworth Park. Most of the village's gritstone buildings are 19th century, built around the needs of the Chatsworth estate, but the former Beeley Hall, with its mullion and transom windows, is one of a number of older properties. The church of St Anne incorporates a Norman door arch and a 14th century tower.

By footpath from the busy B6012 that bypasses the village it is a half-mile walk to Beeley Bridge, sometimes referred to as 'One-arch Bridge'. This is the entrance to Chatsworth Park. Nearby, charming Beeley Lodge stands at the end of a private driveway. The bridge is only wide enough for one-way traffic and so steeply arched that there is no view of any oncoming vehicles on this busy road. It is likely that it was the site of Derbyshire's first traffic lights. What drivers miss beneath the smooth ashlar blocks of the bridge, designed by James Paine and opened in 1760, is the unusual sight of a fence suspended in the river from chains fixed beneath the arch. Its purpose is to prevent deer escaping.

BELPER

Formerly known as 'Beau Repaire', this was once prime hunting territory and was at the centre of extensive parkland and forest where Norman lords pursued the chase. Belper Parks, a small area of open ground around Coppice Brook, is all that remains of the former royal deer park. What happened? In a word, what we like to call 'progress' based on industrial development.

Even in medieval times there were cottage industries. Nail making was a Belper speciality over centuries. Workshops with forges were built in among the houses and at the bottom of gardens, particularly on the slope between Nottingham Road and Parkside. Rumour has it that in these cramped and hot conditions men and women alike sweated and worked stripped to the waist beside glowing furnaces. In the market place, number 31 was once a nail warehouse, one of many dotted around the town. It was a trade that continued here until 100 years ago. Textiles were also an important early business with both the hand spinning of cotton and framework knitting taking place.

Belper was really transformed by one man, Jedediah Strutt, a remarkable individual whose influence on the town in the late 18th century ran deep and is inescapable here even today. Strutt, and therefore Belper, were in on the ground floor of the Industrial Revolution. Jedediah put up the capital that enabled Richard Arkwright to exploit his inventions. As a result, he was able to build only the second water-powered cotton-spinning mill. That original mill, off Bridgefoot, burned down but was immediately replaced using fireproof cast iron instead of timber beams. North Mill, as it was called, still stands and now incorporates the Derwent Valley Visitor Centre. Behind the mill, a high weir flanked by sluices raises the water level and creates an impressive horseshoe waterfall.

Belper grew rapidly with industrialisation. Leaflets are available locally from the Heritage Centre, based in mid 13th century St John's chapel, to guide visitors to the industrial sites. St John's is Belper's oldest building. Other old properties can be picked out by their use of locally quarried pinkish-brown sandstone. Worth a look on St John's Road is the former Robinson's Cotton Mill where yarn was spun by hand. The impact of mechanisation is demonstrated by the fact that less than a decade after Strutt built his first mill Robinson's was bankrupt.

❧ BIG MOOR

―――― The eastern moors — Totley Moss, on the border with South Yorkshire, Big Moor, Ramsley Moor and boggy Leash Fen — were not embraced by the Peak National Park until 1984, over 30 years after the Park was established. Part of the reason was the reluctance of the water authorities to relinquish control of what was an important catchment area. Compared to their western neighbours these moors remain much less well known. It was not until fire swept the area of ground cover in 1959 that significant Bronze Age remains became apparent. There are three stone circles and countless barrows on Big Moor.

Numerous trackways and packhorse routes cross the high moorland. These were once important links connecting the major market centres of Chesterfield and Sheffield with the towns and villages of the Derwent Valley and beyond. At route junctions where paths crossed, stone guideposts were set up and several can be discovered on the moor. Most date from after a 1697 Act of Parliament required crossroads to be marked but some are older. Documentary evidence for Lady's Cross on Big Moor goes back to 1263. This marker was on the saltway from Northwich in Cheshire, via Buxton and the Curbar Gap to Chesterfield. It is no longer a crossroads but for just a short distance the line of the north to south route can be clearly seen crossing today's footpath. A few hundred yards east of Lady's Cross this path joins the B6054. The road was straightened when it became a turnpike in 1759. Turn off the footpath to follow the old trackway parallel to the road 100 yards away and you will arrive at an interesting clam bridge over Bar Brook. Formed by laying two stone slabs side by side such crossings are simple but effective. The blocks laid here each measure about 9 feet in length.

BIRCHINLEE

—— You may struggle to find Birchinlee except on the most detailed of modern maps. Or even for real. There is a fingerpost, high up on Haggside, beside a footpath crossroads between Hagg Farm and Lockerbrook Farm announcing Glossop one way, Birchinlee and Penistone the other, but Birchinlee has all but disappeared. Just the merest ghost remains of this unique village hidden in the woods and rhododendron drifts lining the west bank of the Derwent Reservoir. Better known as 'Tin Town', the village was built a century ago, in corrugated iron, by the water company. Housing was necessary in this remote spot to accommodate the labour force employed on constructing the Howden and Derwent dams and their families. It sounds primitive but this was no squalid shantytown. In fact it had a full complement of Edwardian conveniences, including shops, public baths, sewers, and its own hospital. There were even allotments. Although the 'tin' has vanished the outline of the settlement can still be traced. Severn Trent Water, who are now the site owners, are planning its conservation.

BIRCHOVER

Set in a fold between the high moors of Harthill and Stanton, Birchover is surrounded by impressive natural scenery and some highly unusual man-made additions. The muddle of large rock slabs that stretch along the pinnacle of Rowtor Rocks, behind the Druid Inn, has an amazing suite of chairs, benches, a cave and a square font all sculpted from the natural rock and linked by stone steps. This incredible assortment was the

A three-seater stone bench at Rowtor Rocks, Birchover.

brainchild of local Reverend Thomas Eyre who had the rock carvings made in the 17th century and must have enjoyed entertaining his friends in this highly unusual social setting with such glorious views on offer.

BOLSOVER

——— Bakewell puddings are still very much with us but Bolsover buckles, once equally famous, are now a distant memory. Mining and heavy industry took over in the 19th century.

Work on Bolsover Castle started in 1623 but there had been a fortress on the ridge since Norman times. Now looked after by English Heritage the castle is the main visitor attraction and well worth viewing, but visitors should not miss the less obvious areas of interest. The well house, opposite the magnificent indoor riding school with its Flemish gables, was fed from outside. On a hillside south of the castle four conduit houses stand along the line of an underground spring. In various stages of disrepair they are small, about 10 feet square, but solidly built of stone and with gabled roofs. Further away, across a road to the north-east is a larger conduit house built at the same time as the castle on the site of a spring. Water was pumped from here by hand windlass and later using a horse driven system to the well in the Great Court via lead pipe. Known locally as 'the cundy house' it too is roofless, bedraggled and a little forlorn but still an important snippet of history.

Castle Street leads from the castle to the 'old' town of Bolsover with some attractive stone houses around the market place. Beneath the dramatic ruin of Sir Charles Cavendish's baroque fairy tale castle, New Bolsover goes largely unnoticed by visitors but is a wonderful example of a planned model village.

The Bolsover Colliery Company built 200 terraced cottages in a double row around three sides of a square in the 1890s. New Bolsover was a totally self-contained community with its own school, chapel, policeman, sports ground and a Co-operative store where everyone shopped and earned their 'divi' as the dividend paid to those owning a share was popularly called. Separate from the main properties along Villas Road are the larger, semi-detached houses where the supervisory and senior staff lived.

One of the perks of working down 't'pit' was a coal allowance. This was delivered to the rear of the houses on a tramway and explains why such a wide road runs around the backs of the houses.

It was barely five minutes' walk to the pithead for the miners of New Bolsover, but the colliery has now closed and with it a way of life but something of the community spirit remains.

BONSALL

—— If you are driving along a route called Via Gellia you would expect to be in Rome or Florence but here it is in Derbyshire, running westwards from the A6 below Matlock along the valley of Griffe Grange. Philip Gell of Hopton Hall, with a degree of self-indulgent effrontery, grandly named it with classical allusion after himself and his supposed Roman ancestor Gellius, whose funerary urn was found in West Derbyshire. He had the road built in the 1790s to transport lead ore from his mines to the newly opened canal wharf at Cromford. A side road climbs steeply off the Via Gellia towards Bonsall.

The thin, stony soil of the area made farming hard work and the villagers here turned to lead mining — Bonsall Moor is littered with disused shafts for the most part now safely capped — outwork knitting and the cotton mills for their livelihoods. Over 400 knitting frames on hire from the mill companies once clattered away in top floor rooms spinning silk and cotton yarn into hosiery. I have no idea if that is the origin of the colourful name given to 'Clatterway', an area by a sharp bend just outside the village proper, but it is a nice thought. Either that or the sound of horseshoes striking on stone as the packhorse strings negotiated the steep turn. A textile mill at Clatterway corrupted Via Gellia as the trade name for *viyella*, a material they produced.

Increasing mechanisation and the rise of the factory system all but finished outwork knitting but tall windows, designed to let in as much light as possible, can still be spotted along the upper storeys of houses where the stockingers had their knitting shops. One such house overlooks the old market cross with its shaft set on a 13-stepped circular stone base.

BRACKENFIELD

—— The river Amber was dammed in 1958, near to Ogston Hall, and the valley north of Brackenfield flooded to create Ogston Reservoir. Partly submerged beneath the waters close to the Sailing Club is the site of the Amber Valley Camp School. This opened after the Second World War to give children a taste of country life. The young people who came here and the locals who remember them recall fond memories of the camp.

Brackenfield's church is a couple of minutes' short walk from the southern tip of Ogston Reservoir. It was built in 1856 to serve a growing community centred around the large village green. An ancient but less accessible chapel that had served a more widely scattered community for centuries was finally abandoned.

The ruins of Holy Trinity chapel, now partly hidden among trees high on the slopes of Highoredish Ridge, make an interesting visit. A church was recorded on the site in the Domesday survey of 1086 and a 13th century reference in the documents of Darley Abbey mentions what is now merely a footpath to the church as Churchgate Lane. The remains that can be seen today date back to around 1500. There is a bell turret but no bells. According to tradition these were removed and melted down for ordnance by the Roundheads in the Civil War. By the middle of the 18th century the chapel was already in semi-retirement with only occasional services being held there by the rector from nearby Morton. A little of the fabric from the deserted chapel, including a chancel screen and two old oak chairs of unknown provenance, were rescued and taken to the new church.

In this quiet spot it is hard to imagine large congregations once gathered to worship here. But tradition is maintained by an annual pilgrimage to the ancient chapel on Trinity Sunday.

BRADBOURNE

Bradbourne stands high on a ridge sandwiched by the valleys of Bradbourne Brook and Havenhill Dale. Approaching from Fenny Bentley, look out for Bradbourne's former corn mill, built into the hillside in 1726, on a bend on the right hand side of the B5056, shortly before Mill Road turns off to climb into the village. The tailrace runs under the road to join the brook on the opposite side at Tissington Ford.

All Saints' church, mostly Norman with interesting early carvings around a doorway in the tower, Saxon fragments in the north-eastern corner and a 17th century wall painting, is set back from the road in the village centre. Two impressive private houses, the Old Parsonage and Elizabethan Bradbourne Hall, stand next door to the church. In the churchyard stands a gritstone Saxon cross shaft dating from the early days of Christianity in Derbyshire. Carved, free-standing crosses like these were set up at places where people first gathered to celebrate mass, to hear the gospel preached and where the dead were brought for burial in the shadow of the sacred symbol. There is controversy over the exact age of such crosses but the general consensus tends to the 9th century. Originally the incised shaft would have been topped with a cross. As with handles on china mugs and spouts on teapots the protruding parts are vulnerable and are nearly always the first bits to be knocked off. Bradbourne cross, its carved decoration and crucifixion scene well worn, is fortunate to have survived at all. Until it was recognised and rescued, the two halves were being put to rather more prosaic and practical use forming a 'squeeze stile' into a nearby field.

BRADWELL

As if lead mining was not hazardous enough, 'Bradder' beavers were once made here. These protective beaver skin hats were shaped like a pudding basin and worn by miners who attached a candle to the crowns using a lump of sticky clay. What is dangerous about hat making? Well, before the beaver fur was cut from the skin the individual hairs had to be combined in a process called 'carrotting'. The binding agent employed was nitrate of mercury. Breathing the fumes given off was extremely unhealthy and could lead to brain damage.

Industrial development has left its mark on Bradwell but it still has its attractions with a run of narrow alleyways off its main thoroughfare, one leading to Bagshawe Cavern. Bradwell Dale and Bradwell Edge both have striking rock scenery. There is also a mystery earthwork.

Large sections remain of Grey Ditch, a linear rampart and trench that once extended for half a mile across the full width of the dale north of Bradwell. Excavations show the rampart stood 8 feet high and was 22 feet wide at its base. The ditch was of equal width and a further 6 feet deep. An impressive feat of building thought to date from the 7th or 8th century. But who built it and why? Many historians believe it may simply have been a boundary, a powerful declaration of Mercian dominance. The effort involved does seem a bit over the top for that but there is a precedent in Offa's Dyke.

Another option is that it was built as a defensive battle line and some evidence for this can be conjectured. Local legend tells of an unrecorded Dark Age battle at which King Edwin of Northumbria was captured and subsequently executed. Locals remember the 'Eden Tree' where, according to folklore, Edwin was hung. This tree stood until recently at a spot north of the village near the turn for Brough. Also Bradwell has a 'Gore Lane' and the hill east of Grey Ditch is called 'Rebellion Knoll' for no apparent reason. None of these points makes much of a case alone, but together they begin to add up to, at least, an arguable hypothesis.

BRAILSFORD

Way back in pre-Norman England, Brailsford and neighbouring Ednaston agreed to share a church. A location was chosen halfway between the villages. It is called compromise. Admirable in its way inasmuch as nobody feels hard done by but it also means maximum misery because everyone has a distance to travel. All Saints' has a Saxon cross from those early founding days and still sits surrounded by fields astride the parish boundaries.

Where scattered communities often travelled a distance to attend church, some people brought their canine companions. Well-behaved dogs were tolerated and perhaps the occasional donkey to complete a nativity scene, but that was usually where the line was drawn. Animals were not welcome at divine service. This meant individuals arriving on horseback or by waggon had to make arrangements for their mounts. Exceptionally, there was a church stable, and there is one here — a small, weathered brick building easily ignored by visitors unaware of its original purpose. It was probably as much use to the vicar with his two remote parishes as anyone in the congregation.

BRASSINGTON

A clutch of smoky-grey limestone houses congregate on the hillside south-east of the parish church dedicated to St James. This has been extensively renovated but dates back at least to Norman times and may have Saxon origins. Quarrying activity is unavoidable here but it is an area with a lot to see and explore. Either side of the village are the high outcrops of Harboro' Rocks and Rainster Rocks. The 1,200 feet high plateaux have been occupied from the misty dawn of prehistoric times. A family continued the tradition by living in Harboro' Cave as recently as the 18th century.

Wind and rain have eroded fantastic shapes into rock formations that combine to lend an air of mystery. Human hands too have been at work. At Harboro' Rocks a so-called font, a pulpit and a stone bowl pierced by a drain hole have all excited speculation. Easy to suppose they have a Druidic or possibly early Christian connection. Make your own mind up but just as likely some local squire with time on his hands and a fashionable fascination with antiquarianism carved them out in the 18th century.

BREADSALL

—— The significant cotton and silk textile industries in Derbyshire attracted some interesting spin-off businesses. Before artificially derived alternatives became readily available natural dyes were used. As a result there are some areas surprisingly well stocked with damson trees. Breadsall, on the northern outskirts of Derby, is one. Look out particularly for the orchard next to Brookside Farm.

BRETBY

—— Reached by narrow, leafy lanes, Bretby is tucked away in the south-west corner of the county. The modern village grew up as a largely self-sufficient community around the Earl of Chesterfield's estate in the 19th century. A small cluster of houses includes two former schools and a converted smithy.

Over a gate, in Castle Field, a series of pronounced grassy ridges and ditches can be seen. These earthworks are all that remain of Bretby Castle, a large fortified manor house with two courtyards surrounded by a moat, that occupied the site from the reign of King John until sometime around 1600. Its masonry was probably recycled to provide the raw material for Bretby Hall, a remodelled version of which now stands in landscaped parkland half a mile from the village. A series of footpaths cross the estate passing by a string of jewel-like ponds and clumps of mature mixed woodland.

Behind the small triangular green with its water pump, a short path leads past a set of well-worn stocks to St Wystan's. Inside the Victorian church, a small brass plate remembers Benjamin Disraeli, once a regular guest of the Chesterfields.

Bretby Hall's later owners included Lord Carnarvon who sold the property to help finance the famous expedition in search of the tomb of the Egyptian boy king, Tutankhamun. The last private owner left in the 1920s. After housing an orthopaedic hospital within its grey stone battlements for half a century, the hall and nearby grounds have been redeveloped to provide private residential units.

The well-worn stocks at Bretby.

BRIMINGTON

West Wood separates Brimington Common, reduced to a small recreational area by enclosure in the 19th century, and Staveley. Iron ore deposits and coal seams were worked here over many centuries making it a good place to find evidence of traditional extraction techniques. The popular approach was to dig a shaft through the layer of sandstone to reach the minerals lying perhaps 20 to 40 feet below the surface. Seams were dug out in a gradually widening bowl at the base of the shaft until it became unsafe. Spoil was then roughly shovelled back before the working was abandoned. Men worked in pairs, one in the pit and the other hauling buckets of ore and spoil to the surface. The characteristic shape of the diggings gave them the name 'bell pits'. Mounds with a sunken centre remain in West Wood showing where the pits were sited. It is easy to be nostalgic about the past but this is one hard and dangerous way of earning a living that few must have been sad to see consigned to history.

❧ BUXTON

——— England's highest market town (ignoring a Cumbrian pretender) is probably also its coldest with average daily temperatures a full 5° lower than those enjoyed in London. It must have made the compensation of thermal springs, at around 88° Fahrenheit the equivalent of a modern swimming pool, even more welcome and to our earliest ancestors possibly supernatural. The Romans, who knew a thing or two about taking the waters and keeping the natives on side, called Buxton 'Aquae Arnemetiae', neatly working in a reference to a Celtic goddess. The wells are still dressed and blessed in Derbyshire's unique style each July.

'Higher' Buxton has the Victorian Town Hall and Market Place. St Ann's Well, the site of the baths, the famous Crescent, the Opera House, Pavilion Gardens and the great stables (now converted to the Royal Devonshire Hospital) are all at the lower end of the town at the foot of St Ann's Cliff. Strolling here it is easy to imagine the privileged, dandified world that once made Buxton such a fashionable spa and provided employment for local people. As well as the more obvious jobs such as operating the baths themselves and providing 'hospitality' for the personal needs of visitors and their retinues, up on the nearby heights of Axe Edge men were employed digging peat to supply the mineral baths with mud. The rivers Dove and Wye are both born in the bracing conditions here 1,600 feet above sea level. Axe Edge is a scenic spot with panoramic views over Peakland though perhaps the diggers who toiled on this exposed plateau had other priorities than appreciating the sights.

There is so much to see here that it is no wonder there are some neglected treasures that do not make the guidebooks. I particularly like what might be called the street furnishings. Strange to think that in 1851 there was a public outcry protesting against the local council's proposed rate to pay for gaslights in the streets. Electric lighting came early to Buxton, in 1900. Notice the fluted 19th century cast iron street lamps, the cannon-style bollards and wall mounted lamps in the Crescent. Then there is the decorative wrought ironwork of the canopies laced with glass extending over the pedestrians' heads on the pavement outside the Grove Hotel and along Cavendish Arcade and the sweeping braced curves of the standard lights arching

A wall-mounted street lamp in the Crescent, Buxton.

above Spring Gardens. Best of all are the elaborate lamps, for example beside The Slopes along Hall Bank. These show the punning crest designed by a local architect, Robert Rippon Duke, of a 'buck' on a 'stone' and a quote from Mary, Queen of Scots. Mary suffered with rheumatism and visited Buxton for the waters several times while in the custody of the Earl of Shrewsbury, staying at, what is now, the Old Hall Hotel. On one such trip she scratched a couple of poetic lines on a pane of glass in the window of her room. *Buxtona, qua calidae celebrabere nomine lympha* — 'Buxton, whose fame the warm waters tell'. This quote, and the date 1580, encircles the crest on these particular models. Sad Mary's poignant second line was 'Whom I, perhaps, no more shall see'.

And finally, do not miss the hexagonal pillar-box opposite the Opera House. This dates from 1867 and is the only Victorian letterbox in Derbyshire. Worth sending a postcard at least.

BUXWORTH

Bugsworth was renamed by popular consent to the more aesthetically pleasing 'Buxworth' in the 1920s, around the same time that commercial traffic ceased on the Peak Forest Canal signalling the end for the village's inland port. The canal was built to carry Derbyshire lime and limestone to Lancashire and Cheshire for both agricultural and industrial use. It terminated at Buxworth Basin, as close as practicable to the quarries on the high ground of the Dove Holes area, to which the basin was linked by 6½ miles of the 4 feet 2½ inches gauge iron railtrack of the Peak Forest Tramway. The canal project was driven forward by businessmen with interests in coal and cotton, who intended to be major customers. The opening of the canal, in 1797, turned Buxworth from quiet village to thriving port. Wharves were soon established with rows of limekilns, tramway sidings and large warehouses. Stables were necessary for the horses that hauled waggons on the tramway and towed narrow boats. Typical of the canal's entrepreneurial backers was Samuel Oldknow, who took the opportunity to diversify into boat building and repair.

The Peak Forest Canal triggered the construction of the High Peak Railway to join up with the Cromford Canal on the other side of the Pennines. When that link was established, in 1831, traffic at Buxworth increased. At its busiest the port was loading up to 70 narrow boats every day, each carrying a load of 25 tons. A second arm of the canal was dug to allow another basin to be built at Whaley Bridge.

Intensifying competition from the railways made canal transport uneconomic. Decline was gradual but inevitable. Closed to trade and expensive to maintain, Buxworth Basin began to silt up. Its remaining water was drained in the 1930s. Since then interest in inland waterways as important features of our industrial heritage and also as a leisure resource has revived. Sensitive restoration has now revitalised both Buxworth and Whaley Bridge canal basins.

CALKE

As hidden treasures go, Calke Abbey, built on the site of a former priory between Swadlincote and Derby, was an outstanding gem. It was possibly the best kept secret of all in Derbyshire until the National Trust took it over, initially reluctantly, in 1985. Now it is widely known as a 'time capsule', its crowded contents representing three centuries of the Harpur Crewe family's eccentricities. The baroque home and its collections are open to the public and well worth a visit but there is also much more to see around the house and in the surrounding park. A recently restored 18th century stable block has a display of waggons, farm implements, early horse-drawn fire fighting equipment, and a blacksmith's shop.

On a slight rise, within view of the house, stands St Giles's church. It has a monument to Sir John Harpur and his wife Catherine Crewe set within railings made by Derby's nationally famous ironsmith, Robert Bakewell. The church is a 'peculiar' which means it falls outside diocesan jurisdiction, a legacy of the days before the dissolution of the monasteries when Calke Abbey was home to a group of Austin canons.

The main entrance to Calke Abbey is in Ticknall, but from

Calke village itself a narrow lane leads by a small group of former estate houses to a little car park overlooking Staunton Harold Reservoir. From here there is footpath access for walkers to explore Calke Park with its 500 acres of valleys, ponds and woodland.

CALVER

The flow of the river Derwent is pushed in an eastward curl by the bulk of Hare Knoll under which the village nestles. The exterior of Calver's former cotton mill, built in 1803 by Richard Arkwright, doubled as the prisoner of war stronghold, Schloss Colditz, in a famous 1960s TV series. Set back from the road, the mill's gaunt bulk, recently softened by conversion to residential apartments, can easily pass unnoticed.

Not far from the mill is a reminder of the days prior to the building of the factories. A time when open fields and common grazing was the basis of the rural economy and before the land was enclosed as agricultural change accompanied industrial revolution. Livestock on unfenced land was liable to stray onto arable plots or in from the next village. A locally appointed official, the pinder, was given the job of rounding up stray animals and impounding them in a pinfold. Owners were required to pay a fine for the release of their livestock. Some individuals were almost as ingenious as the inmates of Colditz in devising ways to 'spring' their beasts illegally and pounds were necessarily of sturdy construction. But in many parts of the country pinfolds were fenced by timber or thick thorn hedging and did not survive once they fell out of use. In an area where stone walls are traditional they stand a better chance of enduring and the restored round pinfold in Calver is a fine example of a number that survive in Derbyshire.

CASTLE GRESLEY

So where is the castle? According to contemporary reports it was here, gently decaying, in 1585. All that is left now is a grassy mound and ditch, rarely visited and barely noticed, marking the site of a typical Norman motte and bailey fortification. This is Castle Knob, a vantage point close to the A444, reached by a footpath leading between a row of modern houses. The Gresley family arrived with William the Conqueror but it was some two years after Hastings that the Normans reached Derbyshire and Nigel de Toeni received his reward, a clutch of manors along the Derbyshire/Leicestershire border. The family changed their name and stayed for 28 generations. A hall at Drakelow, not far away on the banks of the river Trent became the family's main home, but in the turbulent early days the castle would have been a necessary stronghold and symbol of power. Bold earthworks on Castle Knob make for a good interpretation of basic motte and bailey design features. On top of the mound a defensive tower would have stood. Around the mound was the bailey, an open space, possibly with outbuildings and ditch. The whole would have been enclosed by a stout wooden palisade.

In more peaceful times a better standard of living beckoned and the castle was abandoned in favour of a family mansion, Drakelow Hall with its 750-acre park and woodland on the banks of the river Trent. This too has now vanished, demolished in the 1950s to make way for an electricity generating power station. Only the former driveway entrance remains, curved walls funnelling in to a pair of sculpted stone gate pillars with a lodge house behind — an incongruous sight with the enormous cooling towers looming in the background.

The contents of Drakelow Hall were auctioned in 1933. Fireplaces, mirrors, oak panelling, friezes and other bits and pieces can still be found in local properties. Appropriately, misericords, wooden brackets fitted beneath choir stalls as supports for those required to stand for long periods (the name derives from the Latin phrase 'Lord have mercy upon us'), went to the church of St George and St Mary. The church, at Castle Gresley's next door namesake Church Gresley, occupies the site of a priory endowed by the Gresley family.

CASTLETON

Castleton is named after Peveril Castle, the Norman stronghold dominating this western end of the Hope Valley. The area is well known for its underground caverns and internationally famous as the source of Blue John stone, a semi-precious banded fluorspar prized from Roman times. Guided tours take parties of visitors into the underground chambers, a subterranean landscape carved in the limestone bedrock by vanished rivers, to view exposed seams of Blue John. Cut and polished stone fashioned into ornaments and jewellery is for sale.

The energetic might like to walk across Treak Cliff where a footpath passes a number of surface diggings. A search in the rubble usually turns up traces of mineral, the crystals reflecting light with a sparkling range of marine-like colours. Finds are exciting but follow good countryside code practice and please do not take them away. Blue John belongs here on Treak Cliff. The only place in the world it can be found.

CHADDESDEN

Modern housing has spilled over what was Chaddesden Common but this suburb of Derby somehow hung on to a small patch of ancient oak woodland and now has its own local nature reserve. Chaddesden Wood is just half a mile by a quarter of a mile at its widest and although the oldest trees are actually aged somewhere between 100 and 200 years the great oaks are the progeny of generations that have grown from little acorns shed here each autumn. Oak woods sustain a rich variety of wildlife and, as with all habitats, continuity is important. This green refuge in the midst of the city comes as a gentle and unexpected pleasure.

CHAPEL-EN-LE-FRITH

At first glance the self-styled 'Capital of the Peak', 4 miles north of Buxton, looks pretty unremarkable. Aside from a couple of 'Historic Old Town this way' street signs, you could drive through Chapel-en-le-Frith without a second glance, thinking it plain, busy and uninspired. The 'Old Town', with its stocks and village cross in the Market Place, cobbled alleys, flights of steps, interesting houses and a church best known as

St Thomas Becket church at Chapel-en-le-Frith.

Derbyshire's answer to the Black Hole of Calcutta, lies hidden on an elevated ridge above the modern road. Incredibly, the former main highway, Terrace Road, is a narrow thoroughfare squeezing between 17th century houses, its sloping cobbled street worn into deep grooves on either side by the passage of countless waggons and coaches.

St Thomas Becket church is on the site of the original chapel in the 'frith' or forest, at the heart of 40 square miles of Royal Forest where once the kings and nobles of England hunted. It has been added to over the years and has elements from different architectural periods. The square tower dates from the early 1700s. At its foot, a weathered gritstone cross shaft that was brought here in 1920 after it was discovered built into the wall of a nearby house. There is both clock and sundial so no excuse to be late for service. The church is most remembered as a temporary gaol. Some 1,500 Scottish supporters of Charles I, captured in battle by the forces of Oliver Cromwell, were incarcerated here, an enforced congregation pending armed escort to prison. The locks and bolts were left fastened for 2 weeks during which time 44 captives perished.

As well as the more obvious sites mentioned above there is much fascinating detail. Market Place links the open market area to the church and the picturesque run of cottages along Church Brow. Almost every building here has a point of interest or a tale to tell. Look out for Black Greyhound cottage and close by a house with the painted stone head of a bull. Both are former inns as was the post office. Overlooking the Market Place, the King's Head was once a brace of farm buildings. Chapel 'Old Town' is small but it is crammed with charm and character.

CHELLASTON

In the Middle Ages, when Chellaston was an independent village, it was famous for its ornamental alabaster, a type of rock that is easy to carve, shows fine detail and can be polished to give a luminous almost translucent glow. Now it is a residential suburb of Derby. One amongst a choice of public houses is the Corner Pin on Swarkestone Road. Viewed from the street it looks ordinary enough but one gable end reveals the exposed and well-worn frame of an original raised wooden cruck, suggesting that the current building disguises a much older structure. The name of the pub is interesting. Although the sign outside shows a skittle it is most probably a reference to the oddly shaped cask that, in the days before metal replaced wood, was made to slot into the space left when beer kegs were laid around the walls of a cellar. A pin is a cask that holds 4½ gallons and making the 'corner pin' was often an apprentice cooper's final challenge.

CHESTERFIELD

—— Viking street names such as Knifesmithgate and Glumangate, the old cobbled Market Place and a thread of narrow yards and lanes give a distinctly ancient feel to this bustling town. Particularly in the Shambles, the old butchery quarter, it is easy to imagine the medieval shops with their wooden shutters and wide counters projecting into the narrow street. From all around there are views of the world famous crooked spire of the 14th century parish church, St Mary and All Saints, the distortion over the centuries probably the result of facing unseasoned timber with a weighty herringbone cover of lead plates.

Almost everyone has seen pictures of the twisted spire but that is no preparation for the striking scale of the building. This is the county's largest church and that famous spire soars to a height of 228 feet. It makes it all too easy to overlook what else is nearby. For example, in the churchyard is the town's first gas lamp. This originally stood in the Market Place and is dated 1824, about the time illuminating gas lamps were beginning to appear in all self-respecting towns and cities. It is well crafted, functional but with tasteful decoration to a design by Joseph Bower, the metal worker responsible for the Weeping Tree fountain in the garden at Chatsworth. In 1881, Chesterfield became the first town in Derbyshire to install electric street lamps in protest against the price of gas. Although incandescent electric lamps had been around for some time it was only in

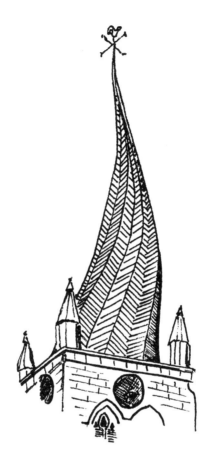

The famous crooked spire of St Mary and All Saints church, Chesterfield.

1879 that Thomas Edison patented the first commercially practical system. Fluorescent electric lamps did not arrive until 1938. As a piece of street furniture this lamp standard is interesting in itself. Now converted to electricity it is also a reminder not only of the days of the nightly lamplighter but also of a spirit of innovation that complements the traditional in Chesterfield.

CHURCH WILNE

—— St Chad's, on the low-lying flood plain close to where the river Derwent meets the river Trent, puts the 'church' in Church Wilne. It has one of the oldest fonts in the country ingeniously adapted from the shaft of a Saxon cross. The church serves the next door village of Draycott and in the past conducted christenings, marriages and funerals for residents of its other near neighbour, Breaston. The track followed by mourners was once popularly known as 'Corpse Way' and led over 'Deadman's Stile'.

CLAY CROSS

—— Less than a decade after father and son George and Robert Stephenson had demonstrated the possibilities for rail travel opened up by their steam locomotive the 'Rocket', George was in Clay Cross surveying a line and laying track to link Derby with Leeds on behalf of the Midland Railway Company. Clay Cross is on a high ridge of land between the Amber and Rother Valleys. The only way to overcome the incline presented was to tunnel beneath. Stephenson, who spent his early working life in coal mining as a fireman and engineer, must have been highly delighted when his navvies struck rich seams of coal and iron during the digging. The result was a profitable little sideline exploited by the newly formed George Stephenson and Co, a business that developed into the Clay Cross Company and turned this rural outpost into an industrial town. Stephenson bought Tapton House, below Castle Hill on the outskirts of Chesterfield, and spent the rest of his life in the area.

The railway tunnels were driven for a distance of a mile beneath Clay Cross. Fifteen million bricks were laid in the process. Nine air shafts provided ventilation, the deepest plunging downwards over 140 feet. The town has seen considerable expansion since the pioneering days of the 1830s but the circular brick columns of the air vents, about 15 feet high, can still be found sprouting incongruously amongst a variety of shops and other properties. Twin rail track disappears underground through a pair of curiously egg-shaped openings — plain and workmanlike at the southern entrance (near Clay Lane) but bedecked with flamboyant round Moorish towers where they emerge to the north. Hidden amidst the modern industrial units that have sprung up around them these ornamental arches look as if they would be more at home in the Alhambra and represent a fascinating if rarely noticed piece of railway history.

The first customers invited to travel through the 'mile-long', as the tunnel was nicknamed, were civic officials and VIPs representing towns along the route from Chesterfield to Derby. Unfortunately there were teething troubles. The inaugural train broke down in the tunnel causing a fair amount of panic and a not very dignified dash for the open air by some of the more claustrophobic dignitaries.

The line is still in use but trains no longer stop at Clay Cross. All that remains of the local station, 1 mile north of the town beside the Tupton to North Wingfield road, is a solitary brick building. This is now in use as a store but refined, matching cast iron window frames offer the observant passer-by a clue to its former status. There was also a station serving Stretton, a mile the other side of Clay Cross. This is now Holly Brook cottage, a private house. Again it is the window, a sweeping arch, of the former waiting room that gives away its railway connection.

Stephenson is the name that everyone remembers but he did not work alone. One other name deserves to be rescued from oblivion. William Howe was employed as a foreman at Stephenson's locomotive works in Newcastle. In 1846, he accepted the offer of a job as Chief Engineer at the Clay Cross works. One of his inventions, a form of locomotive valve gear known as 'link motion', was jointly patented by Howe and Stephenson. It had wide application in many branches of engineering and is still in use today, but technical textbooks seem to have forgotten the modest Mr Howe and remember only his sponsor, George Stephenson. However, William does have his own, very little known but rather special, commemoration at St Bartholomew's church. The vicar of Clay Cross was married to the sister of the celebrated artist William Morris, who with Burne-Jones practically reinvented household design in the 19th century. The connection led to a decorated glass memorial window by Morris, dedicated to the memory of William Howe.

CLOWNE

There is a sense in which the whole of the north-eastern corner of Derbyshire, on the coal belt shared across the border with Nottinghamshire, is 'hidden'. It is an unsung part of the county with attractions that are not always obvious and require some effort to seek out. Clowne is typical of the colliery villages that grew up around the mining industry but there are clues to a more varied past.

Manor Farm, on the edge of the village, is a reminder of the ancient manor recorded in the Domesday Book as, unusually, still in the hands of its Saxon owner 20 years after the Conquest. Next to the farm is Harlesthorpe Dam. Locally this stretch of water is called 'Bump Mill Pond' an interesting name that suggests it was once used to process flax. 'Bump' or 'Bumph' has confusing associations with a range of different linen and cotton by-products, including the manufacture of wicks for tallow candles. Since records show Clowne once had a flourishing sailcloth industry, a material also commonly known as 'Bumph' cloth, it is reasonable to suppose the pond was connected with that trade.

Flax was grown for fibre and also for its seeds that could be ground to extract linseed oil or fed to livestock. In order to allow the central fibre to be separated from the woody part of the stem, flax straw was 'retted' in water. The longest, straightest fibres could then be woven to make a strong linen fabric. Waste fibres, or 'tow', was used as upholstery stuffing. A labour intensive industry, it was doomed once the cotton gin had been invented as it was unable to compete with the cheap, factory produced cotton.

Today this quiet pond is fairly well stocked with fish and popular with the village anglers. But loading the water with rotting straw for a couple of months every year cannot have done the fish population any favours at all in the past.

 ## CODNOR

—— Travelling north along the main road from Ilkeston, town and village — Heanor, Loscoe, Codnor, Ripley — follow each other nose to tail in an unremarkable and barely distinguishable urban sprawl. Easy then to pass through but a glance behind the obvious is rewarding.

Richard, Coeur de Lion granted the manor of Codnor to Sir Henry de Grey as a reward for his loyal resistance to the machinations of Prince John. Grey built a magnificent castle protected by a deep moat in the midst of a 2,000-acre estate. Substantial towers rose at each corner of the curtain wall within which the living quarters were arranged around two large courtyards. The Greys were influential members of the aristocracy. Lady Jane Grey, for nine days Queen of England, who became a tragic pawn in the struggle for power after the death of Henry VIII, was a relative. From the Greys, Codnor Castle passed to the Zouch family who sold the castle in 1634. From then on decay began gradually to set in.

Today, the site has just a few fragile ruins of the once mighty castle and even fewer visitors. When great buildings like this are left abandoned they make a good source of free raw material. You can call it 'robbing' or 'recycling' according to personal preference. A glance at some of the older properties in the vicinity offers a few clues to the whereabouts of some of the vast amount of stone that has disappeared over the centuries.

COTON-IN-THE-ELMS

—— Those pesky little bark beetles that spread the fungus responsible for Dutch Elm disease did for the elms but there is now plenty of tree planting taking place and new woodland springing up courtesy of the ambitious National Forest Project. A brook cuts across the tiny triangular green at the heart of the village where there is usually a small congregation of tame ducks adding to the rural charm of the scene.

The development of the National Forest has attracted visitors to the area but this southerly tip of Derbyshire remains essentially a tranquil corner of the county. Few walkers taking the footpath leading by Malt House Farm to Lullington, a little over a mile away, realise they are treading the 'Procession Way', the route taken by funeral parties before 1846 when Coton acquired a church of its own. Trees form a natural canopy along a stretch of the track bounded by tall hedgerows and gave rise to this section of the coffin route being dubbed 'Devil's Arches'. The squat spire of Lullington's church in the distance has its own inelegant alias. It is familiarly known to locals as the 'spud'.

CROMFORD

Why Cromford? It is 1769. You are an itinerant barber with a bright idea and a driving ambition. In your pocket is the patent to your new invention the water frame, a basis for a water-powered cotton mill. It will be the first of its kind anywhere in the world and signal the start of a factory system leading ultimately to assembly line manufacturing. But Cromford, 2 miles south of Matlock, has few people and transport connections are poor.

The answer is that a reliable, controllable and constant source of water was available and so Cromford became the crucible in which industrial history was forged. Here, in 1771, Richard Arkwright built the first water-powered cotton mill and with it pioneered the techniques of mass production. Events at Cromford may have changed the world but despite its importance it remains a quiet village. The original mill is now owned by the local Arkwright Society who have carried out numerous conservation projects in the area and publish excellent local guides.

Having chosen his location, Arkwright set about solving the problem of labour supply by advertising his jobs widely and building houses to attract workers to the area. Typical is North Street, a cul-de-sac leading off Cromford Hill behind the Market Place, where a terrace of three-storey gritstone properties built by Arkwright has been restored by the Landmark Trust. There is just one room on each floor. The attics housed knitting frames, on which the men in the households wove yarn into stockings while the women, and children from the age of 7, worked 12-hour days at the mill. Arkwright was an enlightened employer by the standards of his day. Sunday schools were set up for the children, and allotments made available at a cheap rent.

Along a footpath at the end of North Street is a walled well known as the 'Bear Pit'. Deep at its foot runs Cromford Sough, dug to drain the water flooding into nearby lead mines but diverted through sluices to help drive the cotton spinning machinery. Originally called Longe Sough, excavation began in the 17th century and took a hundred years to complete. A little lower down the hill it reappears, this time above ground, crossing over Mill Lane by means of a narrow iron aqueduct.

The success of Arkwright's mills slowly influenced improvements in communications but it was the middle of the 19th century before Cromford acquired a railway station. Inspired by cross-channel tastes, the architect employed by the Midland Railway Company (thought to be G.H. Stokes) clearly had fun designing the building on classical French lines, adding a château-style stationmaster's house to complete the illusion. The station is half a mile north-east of the village centre but is well worth the walk if you do not arrive by one of the occasional trains that still operate between Derby and Matlock. On the way, the river Derwent is crossed by a 15th century, former packhorse bridge. At the south-eastern corner of the crossing are the remains of a bridge chapel. Study the bridge from both sides and you will see that each of its trio of arches are pointed on the downstream side but rounded when viewed from upriver. The rounded arches were added when the bridge was widened.

Look out also for an inscription on the bridge recording the daring of local man Benjamin Haywood, who, in 1697, hurdled the parapet on horseback landing safely in the river below. One hopes he took a few quiet moments at the chapel afterwards.

CROMFORD CANAL

The profitability of the first canals began to attract further investment to extend the navigation. Planning for 15 miles of waterway to link Langley Mill on the Erewash Canal to

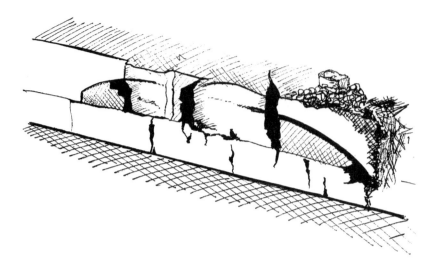

Intriguing niches in the stonework of the Cromford Canal.

Cromford, as the first stage of a connection ultimately to Manchester, began in 1788. It opened to traffic 6 years later. Abandoned in 1944, the waterway is now shallow and overgrown with the exception of a short final stretch between Leawood Tunnel and Cromford Wharf. The towpath provides good walking, rich in wildlife as well as industrial history.

Taking a few hours off from writing this book to stroll in the sunshine I happened to meet a Park Ranger cleaning silt from the canal bed immediately below the road bridge at Whatstandwell. He pointed out two recently discovered matching niches forming an incised arch on the inside edge of the retaining stonework either side of the channel. Perhaps not surprisingly, these faint marks had previously gone unnoticed. Now similarly moulded stonework has been found elsewhere on this waterway and also on the Kennet and Avon Canal. It is possible that near raised embankments, where any breach would result in disastrous loss of water, stop gates capable of being raised into place to form a barrier in an emergency were laid in the bed of the canal. It is an intriguing theory and if true, the evidence may still lie submerged in the deep silt.

DALE

Ringed about by the industrial townships north-east of Derby, Dale has somehow survived as an island of tranquillity in a rising tide of modern urban development. Of the Abbey of St Mary, founded in 1197, all that remains is the archway of the chancel window, although a house nearby incorporates large stone blocks recycled from the original building. The abbey was still being 'quarried' in the 18th century, when the founders of the Moravian settlement at Ockbrook were given permission to remove any remaining reusable remains.

An unusual feature of the small village church is that it is semi-detached, sharing a roof with a neighbouring house. Prior to the Dissolution, the White Canons may have used All Saints' church as an infirmary. Abbey hospitals had their own separate chapel to ensure spiritual as well as medical needs were being met. It is one of two tiny churches in Derbyshire (the other is at Steetley) in which it is claimed Allen-a-dale, minstrel companion of Robin Hood, was married. The house next door was once the Bluebell Inn, conjuring up imaginary scenes of the 'Merry Men' of Sherwood adjourning for a celebratory glass of ale and a hearty singsong.

The church may in fact pre-date the abbey. Local legend claims it was built by the Lord of the Manor impressed by the piety of a local hermit. Follow a short path into the woods behind the church and you will discover the hermitage itself — a cave carved into an outcrop of soft sandstone.

DALE ABBEY

Sited to catch the wind on the skyline of a hill north-west of the village stands the privately owned Cat and Fiddle Windmill complete with four sails and tail post. Not every area had the necessary natural water supply to power water mills and the advent of wind-powered machinery offered a useful alternative from the Middle Ages onward. The Cat and Fiddle mill dates from the 18th century and is a post mill, so named because the design incorporates a main post running vertically through the central spine of the structure. A pair of braced crosstrees resting on stone pillars secures the main post in position. In some post mills these huge supporting timbers were buried in an earth mound for added strength and protection from the elements. Here, the stone pillars have been raised and a stone round house added to give protection, extra support and provide a covered storage area for flour and grain. The business end of the Cat and Fiddle mill, the 'buck', sits on top of the main post. This houses the millstones and the mechanism for transferring power from the sails. It must weigh in the region of fifty tons but could be pivoted into the prevailing wind on two bearings, one at each end of the main post, by raising the entrance steps and pushing on the 'tail'.

DARLEY DALE

—— Considerable development has smeared Darley Dale along and around the A6 north-west of Matlock. Stancliffe Quarries here have supplied gritstone for buildings at Hyde Park Corner as well as for the walls of the Thames Embankment and the Walker Art Gallery in Liverpool. Away from the main road hustle, in an area known separately as Churchtown, 12th century St Helen's church with its famous ancient yew tree overlooks the broad flood plain of the Derwent. Darley Bridge dates back to the 15th century. Maintenance and widening has left two original pointed arches while others have been rounded, reminiscent of the same odd mix at Cromford. Both bridges are of a similar age and so perhaps the same construction team was involved.

Across the bridge, turn right and then fork left to find Clough Wood. Packhorses once came this way and the route they followed is roughly paved with gritstone for part of its width. Walkers should be able to discover the impressive wall of a building hidden in the woods like some ruin from a lost civilisation. Massive masonry blocks frame a 10 feet high arched window. This once housed steam-powered beam engines with enough character to attract names such as 'Jumbo' and 'Baby' pumping up to 30,000 tons of water daily from the shafts of Mill

Close Mine thousands of feet below. In 1931, Mill Close was supplying 90 per cent of the lead produced in Britain and was a contender for the title of richest lead mine in the world. Less than a decade later the battle against the elements had been lost. In1938 a shaft struck into an underground lake and the mine was forced to close down.

🌿 DERBY

───── In common with many expanding cities, Derby has swallowed and urbanised a rural fringe of villages and countryside in its suburbs. An important administrative centre from Roman times, growth really began when the Midland Railway Company chose Derby for its headquarters. The company crest was saved when the old buildings were revamped and can now be seen overlooking the modern station's car park. The railway attracted other business and triggered an industrial boom. However, building Midland station a mile south of the market place changed the focus of life in the town. Derby today still seems to have no natural gravitational centre, making exploration a challenge. A good start to uncovering the city's wide ranging industrial heritage, from silk and iron to locomotives and aeroplane engines, can be made at Derby Industrial Museum, aptly based on the site of England's first silk mill.

But Derby has older treasure in one of only a handful of complete bridge chapels (there are others at St Ives, Cambridgeshire; Bradford-on-Avon, Wiltshire; and Wakefield, Yorkshire) in the country. St Mary-on-the-Bridge, inconspicuously sandwiched between a late 18th century bridge and a reinforced concrete swathe of inner ring road, still stands on its original medieval foundations by the west bank of the river Derwent. One of the original low arches of the lost bridge is clearly visible above ground level in the lower foundations. Bridge chapels were shrewdly placed for spiritual business. When St Mary's first opened its doors, sometime around 1300, this was the only crossing for miles making it 'prayer central' for travellers wishing for a blessing on their journey in such hazardous times. Priests dispensed hospitality in the form of shelter, food and nursing care to those in need and collected alms from the more fortunate. After the Reformation the chapel building was converted to secular uses and a wide variety of tradespeople operated from the premises.

In 1588, the dismembered bodies of three Roman Catholic priests were displayed on the bridge behind the chapel. Nicholas Garlick and Robert Ludlam had been discovered celebrating mass at Padley Manor in the north of the county. A colleague, Robert Simpson, was arrested soon after. It was the wrong time to be caught. The Spanish Armada of 130 ships carrying 24,000 men was threatening to rally Roman Catholic support and overthrow Queen Elizabeth I. Anti-Catholic feeling was at its height. Mary, Queen of Scots, often a prisoner in Derbyshire in the care of the Earl of Shrewsbury, had been beheaded just months earlier. Even so, it was a particularly gruesome event for which the martyrs are now remembered by an annual pilgrimage at Padley.

The importance of St Mary-on-the-Bridge was largely overlooked until the 1930s. Now not only has the structure been renovated but also spiritual ties have been restored through links to nearby Derby Cathedral.

DOVERIDGE

Two centuries ago the turnpike chose to bypass Doveridge, a route itself bypassed by the recently constructed A50 trunk road that crosses the river Dove alongside a graceful medieval bridge that was decommissioned in the 1970s. This double bypass makes Doveridge, though now quite a large residential village with considerable modern development surrounding a few 17th century houses, easy to miss. It is well worth a visit.

On the flood plain between the village and where the bypass carries road traffic across the river, a slender elegant 19th century iron suspension bridge takes walkers across the river Dove, the structure swaying and resonating with each footfall.

The most famous yew tree in Derbyshire grows in St Helen's churchyard at Darley Dale. An equally remarkable tree, and one with a fascinating legend attached, stands beside 13th century St Cuthbert's church in Doveridge. Its canopy, arching over the church path, extends for some 30 yards. Gnarled arthritic branches still full of foliage are now supported by sturdy props.

Yew trees are frequently associated with churchyards. The first missionaries are said to have preached the gospel in their shelter. It is likely that old trees already marked meeting places and grew on sacred or significant pagan sites that were adopted and taken over by the new religion. Long-lived and evergreen, the yew was seen as a symbol of immortality. Branches have been discovered deliberately placed in ancient burial mounds. It has also been suggested that yews were planted near churches to ensure a supply of its compact, springy wood for longbows. A theory supported by the fact that, in the Middle Ages, archery practice took place in churchyards (see Tissington entry). But the raw material for medieval bows was almost all imported from Spain.

According to legend, Robin Hood and Maid Marian were betrothed in the shade of the Doveridge yew. A medieval verse housed in the British Museum records:

'Said Robin Hood, lady fair, whither away,
Oh whither fair lady away?
And she made him answer, to kill a fair buck,
For tomorrow is Titbury day.
When dinner was ended
Sir Roger the parson of Dubbidge
Was sent for in haste;
He brought his mass book, and
He bade them take hands,
And he joined them in marriage full fast.'

The reference to 'Dubbidge' is presumed to be Doveridge. 'Titbury' is Tutbury, a village just a few miles across the border in Staffordshire where an annual fair was held in the Middle Ages.

Because it is slow growing the grain of yew wood is dense. This, and a tendency for the heartwood to decay, makes dating by conventional means such as dendrochronology, in which a sample core is drilled in order to match the pattern of seasonal ring growth against a standard record, difficult. In the absence of confirmatory records estimates have to be based on comparative growth rates. Claims of yew trees approaching two thousand years of age, as at Darley Dale, probably exaggerate the reality. Even so, a thousand years or more is still very conservative guesswork with a venerable specimen like the Doveridge yew.

DRONFIELD

——— North of Chesterfield, close to the border with Sheffield and Yorkshire, Dronfield has developed into a modern small industrial town. Growth based on coal, iron and metalworking did not mean agricultural issues were not important. In towns everywhere, the artificially high price of bread resulting from protectionist taxes on wheat, imposed to safeguard domestic growers after the end of the Napoleonic wars made cheaper imported grain once more available, was a cause of great concern. Prime Minister Robert Peel finally set about creating a free market with the repeal of the Corn Laws in 1846. The people of Dronfield celebrated by erecting a solid gritstone monument with ornamental carvings and a conical roof. Subsidies and artificial prices still feature in agricultural policy and though most people have forgotten all about the Corn Laws, Peel's monument still stands in the market place.

DUFFIELD

——— It is a bit late to be pointing the finger at Robert de Ferrers, Earl of Derby for the loss of a great castle at Duffield. No doubt he had his reasons. Henry III was generally regarded as an ineffectual ruler and not very competent financially. In retrospect though, perhaps the Earl should have counted himself lucky to be let off with a caution and a heavy fine for his part in revolt against the King. When instead he regrouped his forces and once more allied himself with the barons of

England, led by Simon de Montfort, against the Crown he must have known the penalty for failure would be severe. After defeat at the Battle of Chesterfield, Robert was captured, found hiding in Chesterfield church. This time there was no first offence leniency. De Ferrers was dispossessed and his stronghold at Duffield destroyed completely.

The grassy mound where the castle stood is in a splendid strategic position commanding the main road and a historic crossing point of the river Derwent. It is no surprise to learn that this was a fortified site before Henry de Ferrers built a timber motte and bailey stronghold here after the Conquest. A stone castle replaced this at a later date. And what a fortification it must have been. Its massive keep, over 90 feet square with solid walls up to 15 feet thick, put it in the major league of Norman castles. Right up there with the Tower of London.

So effective was the destruction of Duffield Castle that there is little to see on this 5-acre site except for grass and tarmac but it is well worth climbing up the steps that lead from Milford Road just to see the scale of the foundations for the great keep.

EDALE

Each year thousands of pairs of boots arrive in Edale to attempt the Pennine Way courtesy of modern motor transport. It is perhaps hard to believe now but this was a remote place before one of the last major city links, the railway line connecting Sheffield and Manchester, opened along the Hope Valley in the 1890s. Until then, Edale was little more than a loose collection of five 'booths' or enclosed farms that have their origins in temporary hut shelters for shepherds grazing their flocks on the rich summer pasture. Over the years the seasonal havens became permanent farms, labourers' cottages were added and the settlements grew.

The fingers of Edale push into the rugged Kinder plateau where if you are lucky and patient you may be rewarded by the scampering sight of a rare mountain hare. Hunted to extinction in the 19th century they have now been successfully re-established. Derbyshire Wildlife Trust organises an annual

You might be lucky enough to see a mountain hare if you walk in the Edale area.

springtime walk to count sightings. From this and other surveys the current population is estimated at between 500 and 1,000. Smaller than their lowland cousin the brown hare, and with shorter ears, mountain hares are a greyish, almost blue-tinged brown in summer. In winter, except for black ear tips, their fur turns white to blend with the snowscape, a pertinent reminder that this is where the bleak, high altitude north begins. It also makes them particularly conspicuous when there is no lying snow cover. Another rarity associated with the environmental conditions is the cloudberry, a tiny cousin of the blackberry bearing orange berries.

The sites chosen for the early booths make an interesting study in practicalities and reflect the sensitive climatic balance of the area — positioned above any frost pockets on the south-facing ridge of Kinder where there is opportunity to catch maximum sunshine. Not for nothing is the north face of massive Mam Tor, 1,700 feet of rock crowned by a prehistoric hillfort between Edale and Hope, known as 'Coldside'.

EGGINTON

—— The bridges half a mile south of the tiny village of Egginton combine to give a fascinating insight into the history of transport and communications through the ages.

The modern A38 crosses the river Dove (pronounced to rhyme with 'mauve' in these parts) on a platform supported by reinforced concrete pillars. The route broadly follows that of Roman Ryknield Street. A layby on the southbound side makes use of an old stretch of road that loops away to rejoin the carriageway after passing over Monks' Bridge. This four-arched, graceful stone structure has medieval origins, possibly the result of a joint venture between Burton Abbey and the Priory at Tutbury. It is said that one of three bells that hung in the squat tower of St Wilfrid's church at Egginton was sold to pay for essential repairs to the bridge which was widened to carry mail coaches in the 18th century.

Immediately beyond Monks' Bridge stands James Brindley's blue brick aqueduct carrying the Trent and Mersey waterway. At 1¼ miles it is easily the lengthiest aqueduct on England's first long distance canal. The impetus for the development of the canal navigation system came from the Industrial Revolution. James Brindley, born in Derbyshire at Tunstead, near Buxton, was the pioneering engineer who made it possible. Originally known as the 'Grand Trunk', the aim was a waterway that would act as connection to link Hull, London, Bristol, Liverpool and Manchester. For most of its 93 miles the canal follows the contours of the Trent Valley. One of its most important backers was Josiah Wedgwood, who was desperate for an alternative to horse-drawn waggons on roads that had been steadily decaying since Roman times to transport his fragile bone china.

For Brindley, building the Dove aqueduct posed a real problem. His masterstroke was to build half the aqueduct on dry land before diverting the river under the finished section to allow completion of the rest of the structure. This not only facilitated construction but also widened the river, creating a shallower flow and a degree of built-in flood control. This was important because, unlike hump backed road bridges, aqueducts have to be kept flat and as low as possible. All deceptively simple in retrospect but a considerable challenge to the pioneering engineer's ingenuity when faced with the problem in the 1770s. Twelve arches span the river Dove and a further eleven are built into the approach embankment.

Completing the picture of transport through bygone times is a railway bridge crossing the river just a little further south, before the Dove meets the river Trent.

A later addition to Brindley's aqueduct is a FW3/Type 24 pillbox. For obvious security reasons pillboxes were not shown on maps until the very latest published editions. This one is part of a chain of similar fortifications, a thin concrete stop line built in 1940, that can be discovered at strategic intervals along the natural barriers presented by the Trent and Dove rivers. Collectively these defences were intended as last ditch protection of the important routes north; the Rolls Royce aeroplane engine factory at Derby; and of secret munitions

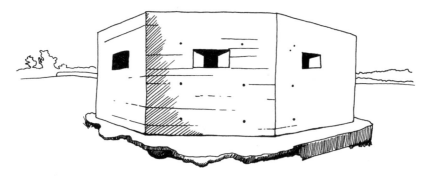

An FW3/Type 24 pillbox added to Brindley's aqueduct near Egginton.

stores in the area. Pillboxes got their name from the characteristic round shape of the early models that proved their worth on the battlefields of the First World War. The FW3 is six sided and designed to accommodate up to seven men: five light machine gunners and two riflemen manning loopholes that command a wide field of view. With such firepower and with walls of 15-inch thick reinforced concrete these pillboxes would have presented a considerable obstacle. Fortunately, by 1941, the threat of invasion had all but disappeared and the pillboxes were not called into use. They stand today as a silent reminder of what was perhaps this country's darkest hour.

ELTON

This is a tiny village but I am sure it would be a good place for radio and television programme makers to consider. It sits astride a marked geological dividing line where limestone meets gritstone shale. As a result the soil conditions vary either side of the main road which should provide some interesting conundrums for the team from *Gardeners' Question Time*.

Judging by the story of Elton's church font, a root around in the parishioners' attics might furnish some interesting material for the *Antiques Roadshow*. When its spire collapsed around 1800, Elton church was rebuilt. Its oddly shaped gritstone font was deemed unworthy of the new building and thrown out. This highly unusual object has a second receptacle, probably a holy water stoup, tacked under the font lip. The smaller container is shown held in the jaws of a carved salamander (not the newt-like amphibian but a mythical beast popularly supposed to be able to survive fire and used as a symbol of virtue) that coils around the base of the font. In profile the stoup gives the font the appearance of a giant lidless teapot. By accident it found its way to nearby Youlgreave as a rainwater receptacle cum garden ornament. Fortunately, the vicar of Youlgreave could recognise a unique 13th century font when he saw one and appropriated it for his church where it now has pride of place in the nave. Leaving the parishioners of Elton to regret their haste and cough up for a replica.

The butting up of grit and limestone at Elton probably caused precious springs to bubble to the surface in sufficient quantity to attract the first settlers on this exposed upland ridge. A fascinating few minutes can be spent exploring various types of dispensers. Behind the church, along appropriately named Well Street, a village pump still stands in a low walled enclosure. It is a manual 'jack pump' with a stone bucket rest of the sort that

The village pump at Elton.

used to familiarly deliver a 'yard of pump water' and was often the focus of village gossip. At least one house nearby also has a well in the back garden, possibly tapping the same source. Pumps of this style could cope with raising water a little over 20 feet so providing the level was not too deep underground it made sense to install a pump. This allowed the well to be covered and prevented the danger of debris falling in and polluting the supply. In Main Street there is a lion-headed cast iron standpipe of the sort popular in late Victorian/Edwardian times, while back in the centre of the village, an old shop front opposite the church has an elaborate hydraulic apparatus attached to an outside wall.

ELVASTON

Derbyshire has a number of notable firsts: the first municipal park; the first national park; and, in 1970 at Elvaston Castle, the first country park. Elvaston, 4 miles south-east of Derby, is not really a castle but a grand manor house that was home to the Earls of Harrington until the 1930s. It is the grounds that attract the visitors: 200 acres of woodland, park, themed gardens, fabulously inventive topiary and a lake. The gardens include rocaille, ornamental rockeries making use of tufa, an unusual material formed by petrification as dissolved limestone builds up layers of rock over lichens and other vegetation. Natural outcrops of tufa occur throughout the White Peak and were the height of garden fashion in the 19th century.

The gardens were the work of William Barron, commissioned by the 4th Earl in 1830. The Earl threw his resources into landscaping the estate and was impatient to enjoy the fruits of his dedication. One of Barron's most remarkable achievements was to successfully transplant mature trees and he managed to move specimens of cedar and other species up to 50 feet high to create an instant pinetum. At one time over 90 gardeners were at work here but as the expense began to take its toll on the Earl's purse their numbers reduced to a mere 11, barely enough to keep the living sculpture of the fancy hedging clipped. The Earl would probably shake his head in disbelief at public access to his wonderful park and gardens. William Barron's instructions were to show no-one around unless Queen Victoria herself should turn up.

Well hidden amongst so many splendid trees at Elvaston, and something of a rarity north of the river Trent, is a large clump of mistletoe. As an evergreen plant, a feature that along with its seemingly magical parasitic habit of living in the air made it of special significance to the Druids, it is easiest to spot in the winter when deciduous branches have no leaves to cloak its presence. Mistletoe tends to favour apple, hawthorn, lime and poplar. At Elvaston it is high on a lime tree. No more clues!

ETWALL

—— What happened if you fell on hard times in the days after the Reformation and before the advent of national state welfare arrangements? From 1557, in Etwall, if you were extremely lucky, of good character and single you might qualify for free lodging and an allowance for food and clothing in one of half a dozen almshouses. These were the charitable gift of the local squire, Sir John Port. The Port family had profited from the Dissolution by acquiring extensive former church property at Etwall, so in many ways it was fitting that they assumed some responsibility for helping the poor and needy.

The almshouses were remodelled and extended in 1681. Internal modernisation has kept pace with the times and more enlightened views allowed married couples. Until the 1960s residents maintained the custom of wearing cloth hats and blue cloaks embroidered with the John Port crest. Over a central arched entrance porch coats of arms are set in the stonework representing the Gerrard, Hastings and Stanhope families, all linked to the Ports by marriage. From the outside the picture the houses present, attractively grouped around three sides of a secluded courtyard beside the parish church, has altered little over the intervening years.

One thing that has changed is the addition of a splendid pair of eye-catching ornamental gates in 1984. Commissioned by Rowland Cotton from Derby's master ironsmith, Robert

Bakewell, to grace the entrance of Etwall Hall early in the 18th century, they feature the hawk and buckle crest of the Cotton family. Incredibly the gates were discarded when the hall was demolished in 1955. They were dumped and left to rust until their value and artistry was recognised by a group of local people who rescued and restored them.

The almshouses form part of a characterful centre to a village that has grown considerably in recent years with Toyota's car factory next door and easy commuting to Derby.

EYAM

Pronounced as a single syllable to rhyme with 'dream', Eyam is a handsome, thriving village with shops, post office and public house. The sandstone bulwark of Eyam Edge provides a protective backdrop to the north. It is well known for the heroic community spirit that, in 1665, voluntarily imposed a strict quarantine on the entire village in order to contain an outbreak of bubonic plague during which more than two thirds of the population perished. Or was it plague? Alternative theories have been proposed suggesting it could possibly have been anthrax or even measles.

Much of the 17th century village remains including three cottages near the church where the early victims lived. There is much to see here and Eyam caters well for its visitors with a museum and plaques around the village to direct and explain everything. Plague cottages (where the first victims lived); a bull ring (bull baiting took place until the 1830s); the water troughs that in 1588 were part of one of the first public water supplies in the country; the carved slab above the Miners' Arms denoting a lead miners' barmote court (see Wirksworth entry); the fine Saxon cross in the churchyard — all are signposted.

One unusual if not unique sight you may miss is a vertical sundial set low down over a side entrance to St Lawrence's church where it is half-masked by a pair of substantial clipped yews. To work accurately the gnomon on a wall-mounted sundial has to make an angle with the dial plane equal to the co-latitude of the site. For example, Eyam is 53 degrees north, so the angle between the gnomon and the face of the dial should be 37 degrees. To read the shadow you need to know that the noon line runs vertically downwards from the centre of the dial with the morning hours on the left and the evening hours on the right. This dial is made to show 7 am to 6 pm with half-hours marked. Interestingly, it also shows noon at various exotic locations around the world and information allowing for the changing inclination of the sun through the seasons of the year. Simple shadow clocks were recorded in ancient Egypt over 3,000 years ago and sundials are mentioned in the Old Testament Book of Kings. Tables were once used to convert solar time to standard time. Now we just look at our digital watches. This fascinating piece of workmanship is said to date from 1775 and is a gem not to be missed.

FENNY BENTLEY

Fenny Bentley sits at the southern limit of the Peak Park astride the Ashbourne to Buxton road — village and church to the west of the A515; old Bentley Hall, now Cherry Orchard Farm, to the east. A square defensive tower of three storeys, similar to the 'pele' towers built on the northern borders of

Old Bentley Hall at Fenny Bentley.

England to counter the threat of cattle and sheep stealing raids by Scots bandits, known as reivers, survives from medieval Bentley Hall. It would originally have acted as a gatehouse guarding the manor enclosure but is now incorporated in the farmhouse and is the probably the only example of its kind in Derbyshire.

The route followed by the London and North Western Railway Company runs to the west of the village and is now popular with walkers and cyclists as the Tissington Trail. Hidden in trees where a goods station operated until 1963 can be found the rusting remains of sidings, signal cranks, points and a gradient post.

 ## FLAGG

—— Behind a collection of houses stretching out along Main Road are a series of narrow arable field strips. Enclosed in early times by drystone walls they are similar to the medieval field strips at neighbouring Chelmorton though not nearly as well known. Flagg's elevated position on quick draining limestone make it an ideal location for the point to point races organised each Easter by the High Peak and North East Cheshire Drag Hunts.

Limestone puts the 'white' in White Peak and has been burned to produce lime here for centuries. Lime mortar and lime plaster were uncovered when the Roman baths at Buxton were excavated. The potential of lime to improve and enrich poor soil has been known from at least the 13th century and probably earlier. When the Industrial Revolution drove up the demand for food, farmers were under pressure to cultivate poorer land and in the Peak District almost every farm soon had a kiln to service its needs and in some cases to earn a little extra from selling any surplus. In most cases farmers built their own kilns to a common 'pudding pie' design with an open topped shaft tapering to an extraction flue at the base. Limestone was loaded at the top along with layers of wood, furze, coal or whatever was to hand to burn. As it melted the lime ran to the foot of the kiln ready to be dug out. Although disused for many years the vestiges of kilns remain to be found throughout the White Peak. In a field north of Flagg Lane can be seen a fine example of a double kiln.

FOREMARK

—— You could be forgiven for overlooking Foremark. Its impressive Georgian mansion and a handful of houses are set back from the minor road that threads along a ridge bordering the Trent Valley. Until 1940 Foremark Hall had been the home of the Burdett family for nearly three and a half centuries. The beautifully balanced proportions of the classic Palladian style mansion commissioned by Sir Robert, the 4th Baronet, in 1760, now house a preparatory wing of the public school at nearby Repton.

Although private property, a footpath crosses the wooded grounds, passing a small lake and giving a good view of the front of the house with four impressive columns dominating the main entrance.

Just outside the hall grounds to the west stands St Saviour's church. Built in traditional style, by Sir Francis Burdett, this was one of the first new church properties to be approved after a ban, imposed by the Puritan inspired Commonwealth presided over by Oliver Cromwell, was lifted. Internally, the church remains largely unchanged from the time it was constructed in the 1660s with box pews and a three-deck pulpit.

Eastwards from the hall, the footpath leads by a row of weatherboarded houses along a chestnut lined track towards Heath Wood. A thousand years ago this was border country where Saxons fought to stem the tide of Danish invasion. Close by, Repton was the administrative centre of the Saxon kingdom of Mercia. King Burgred chose to make his stand at Foremark but the Danes prevailed and Repton was looted. Burgred, a Christian, fled to Rome. In a field just before Heath Wood, a single rank of tall conifers stands sentinel around an oblong barrow. Here lie the mortal remains of the Danes who fell in the battle. Their spirits, according to Viking warrior belief, feast with the Gods in Valhalla.

FROGGATT EDGE

 Derbyshire has its share of henge monuments and stone circles spanning Neolithic times and the Bronze Age. Arbor Low, west of Youlgreave, is the largest and the best known. And if you believe in ley lines, Arbor Low is either communications control or spaghetti junction. Built much later and smaller in scale is Nine Ladies on Stanton Moor. There is no public access to Nine Stones circle on Harthill Moor although there is a good view from the Limestone Way footpath.

 All these monuments attract visitors but even at Arbor Low you are unlikely to find a crowd unless it is the summer solstice or some other special occasion. However, if you would like to explore a little known stone circle in total peace and quiet opt for Froggatt Edge. At 900 feet this escarpment towers over Froggatt village and the Derwent Valley. The geological mix of sandstone and grits of the Edge weather differently producing rocky outcrops of fantastical and strange contours. To the east, across a mile of flat moorland, rises White Edge a full 100 feet higher. Unlike the spruced-up, clean-cut lines of Nine Ladies, the stone circle here is half swamped by bracken and easily missed. The tallest stone is 3 feet 6 inches high, taller than any at Nine Ladies, and stands to the side of what appears to be a southern entrance. The rest of the stones are smaller and somewhat jumbled but the shape of the ring is clear and a matching access point can be made out directly opposite the tallest stone. It is very difficult to date these circles but the size and construction suggest Bronze Age. Why our ancestors chose these lonely high moors for their monuments and the purpose they served remains hidden to us. Clearly, the precision of their astronomical alignment is no accident but we can only guess at what went on here three millennia ago.

GARDOM'S EDGE

 High above Baslow is Gardom's Edge, an area covered with traces of old field patterns and numerous prehistoric cairns. A replica marks the place where a stone was found engraved with small bowl-like depressions surrounded by incised circles. Known to the archaeological fraternity as 'cup and ring' markings their meaning remains a mystery. Using the natural escarpment as one boundary a D-shaped boulder-strewn enclosure is defined by a substantial earth and stonework bank, some 650 yards long with obvious entrances at intervals. What is fascinating is that the enclosure pre-dates the prehistoric field patterns that overlay the site. Was it a pound to keep livestock safe? A fort? A settlement where prehistoric people built their roundhouse huts behind the protective shelter of the bulwarks? A recent theory, backed to an extent by the lack of finds that would normally be expected on a site associated with long habitation, suggests it perhaps served more social or ceremonial purposes as a common meeting place or trading centre.

GLOSSOP

—— Glossop offers two towns for the price of one. The planned Victorian new town of Bernard Howard, 12th Duke of Norfolk, designed to service a once flourishing textile industry is what most people know. Do not miss 'Old' Glossop with which it merges to the east. The old town centre with its market cross in a now tranquil square grew up as part of the estate belonging to Basingwerk Abbey, a Cistercian order with a mother house in Wales. As the focus of the town shifted inevitably to 'Howard Town' with its burgeoning cotton industry it left these mostly 17th century monochrome gritstone cottages in peace. You will find them nestling quietly under the north-western edge of the lofty moors of the High Peak and the barren beauty of wild Kinder Scout plateau, the highest point in Derbyshire.

Kinder is one of the county's most popular destinations. Tourists are attracted by peaks rising beyond 2,000 feet high and picturesque valleys known as 'cloughs'. Less frequented countryside can be discovered on the moors south-west and crossed by Monk's Road which leaves the A624 a couple of miles south of Glossop, heading for Charlesworth. Thirteenth century records show this as 'the Causeway', indicating that the route was important enough to be paved in those early times. Just off Monk's Road, not far from the junction with the A624, is the Abbot's'Chair. This 3 feet by 2 feet solid block of gritstone is 28 inches high and has a 6-inch deep carved 'seat'. From this seat the abbot of Basingwerk Abbey is reputed to have held open-air court for the abbey's remote Glossop manor tenants. Modern opinion is more prosaic and suggests it is most likely to be the base for a medieval cross shaft. I am not so sure. Call me an old romantic but it is the right size for a seat with enough height to lend an incumbent some eminence and signs of wear at the front edge are consistent with repeated use beyond the odd passer-by just trying it out.

Robin Hood's Picking Rods at Cown Edge near Glossop.

A couple of miles west, beside a footpath across Cown Edge, is another unusual piece of stonework. Two large columns, one higher than the other, stand upright in sockets drilled out of a rectangular slab of rock. Again the original purpose of this unique feature is a mystery lost in time. It may have been to brace a longbow for stringing and this would connect it to its local name of 'Robin Hood's Picking Rods'.

GRANGEMILL

What were our roads like before the Romans came? Probably not as bad as we might be inclined to believe. Julius Caesar and Tacitus both remarked on the expertise and skill of British charioteers. If you think about it, reasonably decent trackways must have existed to allow such proficiency to develop.

Numerous ancient tracks cross Derbyshire. Many, on ridgeway routes following the safer higher ground, link henge and other Neolithic monuments and are guarded at intervals by hillforts. From Grangemill, more of a crowded road junction than a village, a footpath climbs a valley to the south where, after half a mile or so, it leads on to a broad green track known as 'Chariot Way'. Has its name survived through time and the generations? The Way is undoubtedly ancient. Part of a prehistoric route that became known as the 'Portway' in Saxon times. Here leading from Wirksworth through Grangemill and from there probably northwards along the course now overlaid by the B5056 to Winster and beyond. Standing alone on Chariot Way on a misty morning it is easy to roll back the centuries and imagine a woad-painted Brigantian charioteer thundering by steering a brace of stocky, wild-eyed native ponies.

GREAT LONGSTONE

People come to Monsal Head just for the view. To gaze at the spectacular panorama of Monsal Dale and maybe walk a little way along the Monsal Trail before heading elsewhere. Just to the east of this famous beauty spot are Great Longstone and its smaller companion Little Longstone, attractive villages of stone houses with the exception of Longstone Hall which is built of red brick.

Great Longstone church has carvings of a milkmaid and a miner, a symbolic combination neatly encapsulating so much of the White Peak. Lead was mined in the rakes of Longstone Edge but also something more unusual. A tough black mineral of the silica family, chert, was also quarried. It is found here and along a short stretch of the Wye Valley from Ashford-in-the-Water to Bakewell. Small pieces can be found loose in scree, more substantial quantities run in seams through the limestone.

Chert was exploited in Neolithic times as an alternative to flint for making tools and weapons. Perhaps not quite so easily workable as flint it could still be flaked into equally durable sharp-edged angular fragments for use as scrapers or knife blades. Larger pieces could be chipped and worked to form axe heads. Chert implements have been discovered over a wide area. The mineral became a commercial proposition late in the 18th century when the Staffordshire pottery industry was expanding. Josiah Wedgwood's factory had a growing demand for their white porcelain and creamware for which one of the main ingredients was flint, ground to a powder between granite rollers. During this process particles of granite dust contaminated the mix causing unacceptable colour variations and blemishes to appear when the pots were fired. Chert grindstones did the job just as well without any of the discolouring side effects.

Lanes and footpaths cross from the village to Longstone Edge, an area dotted with the evidence of, mostly opencast, quarrying activity. And while I am not promising scenic drama of Monsal Dale grandeur there are magnificent views over Longstone Moor and the likelihood is you will have them to yourself.

HADDON HALL

Centuries ago a dust blanket of neglect was thrown over Haddon Hall. It remained effectively mothballed, its medieval integrity intact, maintained but not lived in until the 9th Duke of Rutland blew away the cobwebs and turned Haddon once more into a home. The house is now regularly open to visitors from spring through to autumn and is very much on the tourist trail. Of all the rooms the Great Hall, dating from around 1370 with its flagstones, oak panelling and minstrels' gallery, most summons up the spirit of the Middle Ages: hearty communal banquets and roaring log fires.

A detail that is all too easy to miss is a small metal shackle secured to the woodwork by the entrance. Tradition tells that any medieval banquet guest proving to be insufficiently entertaining, or failing to keep pace with the carousing, was liable to be manacled here. For the rest of the festivities and for the general entertainment of other guests the victim then suffered the indignity of having drinks poured down their sleeve. Oh well, I guess you had to be there.

HANDLEY

West Handley, Nether Handley and Middle Handley make up this scattered rural community north-east of Chesterfield. 'Murder' field on the edge of Middle Handley earned its gruesome soubriquet in 1873. The body of 23 year old Eliza Hudson was discovered here following reports of a violent argument with her husband. Benjamin Hudson was tried, convicted and paid the ultimate penalty at Derby gaol, making history in the process by becoming the first person to be executed behind closed doors at the prison. Previously, hangings were considered a spectator sport.

❧ HARTHILL MOOR

—— Flights of fancy have imagined much in the fantastic shapes into which the gritstone ridges of Harthill Moor have been eroded over time by the forces of nature. This is reflected in names such as 'Mock Beggar's Hall' or 'Robin Hood's Stride'. There are fine views of the silhouettes created on the tors and out over the Wye Valley. The moor has escaped the ravages of quarrying better than its gritstone island neighbour, Stanton Moor, and remains largely untouched by modern man. Footpaths over the moor pass close to the partly ploughed out but still visible earthworks of an Iron Age hillfort known as 'Castle Ring', a single standing stone and Nine Stones, a Bronze Age stone circle. The circle is short of its full complement of stones but those that remain stand an impressive 6 feet high with probably as much as another 4 feet sunk below ground. Some of the gateposts on the moor bear the hallmarks of a bit of opportunistic recycling in the more recent past. I suspect that if it were possible to bring back one of the prehistoric henge builders for an identity parade to try and find some missing stones a likely line-up could soon be put together.

Far less immediately visible is a later addition to the Moor. Scraped into Cratcliffe Tor, its entrance concealed behind the deep green foliage of ancient yew branches, is a hermit's cave. Look inside behind the protective railing. There is a stone bench hewn out of the rock. A small niche presumably held a tallow candle. On the right hand wall, carved in low relief, is a crucifixion scene some 4 feet high. The features are worn and the lower part of the legs damaged, but otherwise the sculpture is in remarkable condition for something that was probably worked with simple tools as long ago as the 14th century. Who the hermit was who chose this lonely spot to contemplate things spiritual away from the temptations of the flesh we do not know. A record survives in the kitchen notes of Haddon Hall to show a possible resident in 1549. A payment was made, on 23 December, to 'Ye harmytt' for supplying ten rabbits. Intended, no doubt, to form part of a typically expansive Tudor Christmas feast.

HARTSHORNE

—— Repton Brook rises close to Hartshorne. Along its short, 6-mile run through the south Derbyshire countryside to join the river Trent, some half dozen or so mill sites have been tentatively identified. Only one site, the first mill on the brook, just half a mile from its source, still has something to show. This mill was originally, and again before it closed in the 1940s, used for grinding corn. In between it was converted for iron smelting and in its most productive phase, from around 1780 to the middle of the 19th century, the rather more unusual job of manufacturing some of the earliest commercial screws. The current building probably dates from this phase in the mill's working life.

The screws produced here were of the type we call today 'self-tapping', made to a patent owned by an engineer from nearby Burton upon Trent, William Wyatt. Holes to receive these screws had to be pre-drilled to size. As the screw was turned it cut the receiving thread. The rector of St Peter's church at Hartshorne, Reverend Stebbing Shaw, a keen historian, recorded 59 people working at the screw mill, including children, in 1796. The waterwheel at that time was driving 36 engines and production averaged 1,200 gross of screws per week.

The mill building was rescued from dereliction in the 1980s and has been converted into a public house and restaurant. Although in a poor state the undershot waterwheel, 4 feet wide and 24 feet in diameter, has been exceptionally well restored and is one of the best to be seen anywhere. It is no longer turned by water power, the dam and mill pond where the water was collected have both now gone, but the illusion is maintained as it turns in its wheel-pit courtesy of a small electric engine.

HASSOP

—— Staunch Roman Catholics even during times when practising their faith carried both the threat and reality of persecution, the Eyre family managed to dominate Hassop from the 15th to the 19th centuries. Sheep farming, lead mining and astute marriage alliances consolidated a family fortune. Hassop Hall, solid and well proportioned but plain, is concealed from the village behind a high wall. This was one of many large Eyre family properties in the area and has now been converted into a hotel.

The church of All Saints faces the hall entrance and is all too easily missed, particularly if you are driving through. Built by the Eyres during the Regency in the style of a classical temple complete with colonnade, it is just not what you expect to see at the centre of a tiny Derbyshire village.

HAYFIELD

—— On Kinder Road by Bowden Bridge is the disused quarry where ramblers protesting against the lack of access to the moors gathered in 1932 for a mass trespass on Kinder Scout. A popular walk from Hayfield starts here joining up with the Pennine Way just before the steep steps of Jacob's Ladder and the descent into Edale. According to tradition, Jacob's Ladder is named after Jacob Marshall who laid the original steps in the 17th century. The tiny one-arched bridge here is little more than 2 feet wide. Instead of the ladder take the detour and look out for the ruins of Edale Head house where Jacob Marshall may have lived. An isolated spot for habitation it was probably intended as a kind of service station and 'refuelling' stop for passing packhorse trains. The last inhabitant left here in 1894.

Although Hayfield to Edale is a well-trodden path many walkers miss the significance of Edale Cross, sometimes called Champion Cross, a corruption of the French 'champagne' or Norman English 'champayne'. This medieval boundary marker is tucked into a recess in the stone wall, shortly after fording the fledgling river Sett, once the power source for Hayfield's textile and paper mills. The cross marks ward limits in the former Royal Forest of the Peak. This hunting preserve of Norman kings was subject to stern forest law and the cross is a potent symbol of the administrative jurisdiction of the forest courts. It is worth stopping here, for in the right conditions there is a fine view of Kinder Downfall, 2 miles north, spray clouds

poised in the air as the cascade heads down into Mermaids Pool
out of sight in the valley below.

HEAGE

North of Derby the A38 steers through undistinguished
countryside deliberately avoiding the built up areas on either
side. The chief Saxon route through the county, the Portway,
once linked the string of towns and villages to the west while
those to the east are on the line of Roman Ryknield Street. Where
the modern dual carriageway bypasses Heage to cut neatly
between Belper and Ripley, travellers may notice two squat
towers in an otherwise featureless roadside field. This is Morley
Park and it once presented a very different scene. What is now
a grassy field was a foundry complex of coke ovens and iron
casting sheds interconnected by a web of tramlines. The stubby
towers are the remains of the first coke-fired blast furnaces in
Derbyshire.

Iron furnaces in Morley Park near Heage.

The A38 is not a place to stop and stare, but head for Heage and you leave the hustle and traffic behind. A fork off the Ripley to Ambergate road climbs steeply up a 1 in 10 incline. Immediately the landscape changes. From this loftier perspective a patchwork of hedged fields mount the horizon and the ribbon of busy tarmac, though barely half a mile distant, fades. Clustered around the crossroads at the centre of Heage, is an interesting collection of old houses. Different styles of stone and brickwork showing different stages of repair and rebuilding through the generations. Behind the church, on Dungeley Hill, there is a fine restored tower mill with a distinctive ogee cap known locally as 'Ned's Mill'. A good view can be had from the footpath but visits are only by prior arrangement. Tower mills were an 18th century design improvement on post mills (see Dale Abbey). Instead of the whole mill having to turn in order to catch the prevailing wind the sails, six in this case, were mounted in a rotating cap.

From the south-east corner of the village footpaths close by Parkside Farm lead back towards the A38 and the remains of the blast furnaces. Morley Park Ironworks were an expansion of Francis Hurt's existing works at Alderwasley, on the other side of the Amber Valley. The Hurt family business had been connected to the lead industry. Francis spotted an emerging market for mill machinery and set up an ironworks near the family home. But given a choice, someone else's backyard is always preferable than your own when it comes to an iron foundry, and so Morley Park was developed with a single blast furnace in 1780. A second was added in 1825. The blast furnaces combine sandstone and gritstone in their construction. Iron ore, limestone and coke were loaded from the top, a job made easier by setting the furnaces into a raised bank. Steam engines blew cold air creating a draught to draw the fired mix and generate temperatures high enough to smelt the ore. Pig iron was tapped and run off from the base. As the furnace roared more ingredients were added to maintain a continuous process. Increasing competition brought it all to an end in 1874. Apart from the furnaces, silent witnesses now beside the new road, the site has reverted to grassland.

⚘ HIGHAM

―――― Higham, with a mix of fine old Jacobean, Queen Anne and Georgian buildings, stands out as a stone built village in the mostly modern, red-brick housing around Alfreton. Travellers miss these delightful properties because the modern A61 trunk road now passes by rather than through the village. In the past, Higham's fortunes were inextricably linked to the passing trade that resulted from its position on what was then a major route through the county, following the line of Roman Ryknield Street. When the turnpike trust set up to ensure improvements to the road diverted the route via Alfreton the whole character of the village changed. If you are sharp-eyed and alert a number of original turnpike cast iron milestones can still be seen along the route ― most of them made locally at James Haywood's Phoenix factory in Derby.

Now transformed into Black Bull Farm, the Black Bull Inn was for centuries an important staging post. In the days of coach travel this was halfway house between Derby and Sheffield, where horses were changed and travellers took refreshment. It also served as courthouse and general hub of village life. Trade was sufficient to keep no less than six public houses in business along the 600 yards stretch of Higham's main street. The local market cross may be a replica rather than the original but it still serves as a reminder of the village's former glory days.

⚘ HIGH PEAK TRAIL

―――― Odd as it seems, the 33 miles of the Cromford and High Peak Railway, opened in 1831, was conceived as part of the canal system. Even the stations were called wharves. It was designed to link the Cromford Canal to the Peak Forest Canal from where there was access to the developing industrial towns of Lancashire. For the engineer, Josias Jessop, it posed considerable problems. In railway terms it was a route of sharp bends and giddying gradients ― 1 in 14 on the lengthy Hopton incline ― and twice as steep for short stretches elsewhere. Before more powerful locomotives took over, horsepower and steam winding engines were employed to haul waggons up the challenging slopes. In the early days the journey was slow. Trains averaged little more than 2 miles per hour. Almost as soon as it was constructed the viability of the railway was questioned. Its ability to generate income was dependent on the success of the canal system. Direct rail freight was already superseding the waterways by the 1830s.

In the search for customers the railway encouraged various enterprises to set up along its length. Relics of these remain along the route, which now forms the High Peak Trail. Some, such as the cliff face scars of a quarry immediately beside the track, are obvious. Others need to be searched out. A mile south of the Minninglow car park, on the High Peak Trail near Pikehall, is the tree-crowned summit of Minninglow itself where a Neolithic chambered tomb overlooks an old packhorse route. Close by the spot where the old track crosses the High Peak Trail is the site of a 19th century brick making operation. The bases of two kilns with vents, flue openings and refractory lining can still be traced amongst the undergrowth and brambles where bricks were fired. Below the embankment can be seen the pits dug to supply the raw clay. High silica content in the local clay produced bricks that could resist high temperatures. Some of the bricks made here were transported to line the steel furnaces of Sheffield.

The axe that fell on several small railway lines in the 1960s is in many ways regrettable. On the plus side, it has provided mini-habitats for wildlife, popular trails for walkers and cyclists and access to some interesting and little known sites — if you know where to look.

HOLYMOORSIDE

—— You cannot seem to go far in Derbyshire without tripping over relics of the lead smelting that was carried out continuously from Roman to modern times. From open hearth 'boles' that are little more than shallow depressions on exposed hilltops, to more sophisticated operations, the signs are all around. In a remote spot beside the B5057, Darley Road, Stone Edge Cupola is the best preserved of the later industrial sites. Passing travellers will notice the square, tapering chimney rising beside the road but unless they are well versed in the sort of trivia in which the *Guinness Book of Records* specialises may well not realise its significance. At 55 feet and popularly known as the 'Pig of Lead', this is Britain's oldest free-standing chimney, built in 1770. Lead was produced here until late in the 19th century employing the reverberatory system in which ore was kept in a closed furnace separate from the fuel. Reflecting heat that would be lost from an open kiln back into the furnace made for a much more efficient process. A flue system connected the chimney to the furnaces and height was necessary to ensure sufficient draught to fire the coals without having to introduce supplementary bellows.

When these smelting works were at their peak of production, under the ownership of Barker and Williamson around 1800, 10 tons of lead per week were passing through the gates for use in plumbing, roofing and other processes — a scale of operations that left a fair amount of waste and slag as the spoil heaps show. Lead smelting was far from an environmentally friendly process but at least the works were sited away from where people were living. Men from Holymoorside would have walked the couple of miles to work here along Harewood Road before cutting through Corporation Wood, crossing a footbridge over the tiny river Hipper to follow a stream to Stonehay Farm and then on to Darley Road. The stone water pumping station in Corporation Wood is a 20th century addition that closed in the 1970s.

Stone Edge Cupola may not be pretty but it is well conserved and represents an outstanding slice of industrial archaeology.

HOPTON

——— When Hopton Hall was sold in 1989 it ended a six centuries old connection between the village and generations of the Gell family. The Gells feature prominently in the history of Derbyshire with individuals achieving prominence variously as soldiers, scholars and industrialists. Sir Philip Gell provided the almshouses for the poor of Hopton and neighbouring Carsington in 1722.

A new road to the south of both villages was built at the same time as Carsington Reservoir and so many people now drive by Hopton and miss the red-brick crinkle-crankle wall that maintains the privacy of the hall. Alcoves created in the wave of the wall are designed as suntraps. Supplemented by hot air blasted from a stove through vents in the brickwork this was the perfect environment for growing and ripening fruit. This particular wall was the inspiration for the Serpentine Walk, a beech hedge planted at Chatsworth in 1953 to frame the approach to a bronze bust of the 6th Duke of Devonshire — the 'Bachelor Duke'.

HORSLEY

Despite being within roaring distance of the A38 trunk road north of Derby and considerable new housing growth on the village outskirts, the centre of Horsley is still relatively quiet and peaceful. The 13th century parish church, St Clement's, has a splendid broach-spire (visible from the A38) in which octagon and pyramid shapes interact. Battlements, added in the 15th century, failed to protect the church from a troop of local volunteers formed to counter the threat of an invasion by the conquering French army of Napoleon Bonaparte. Visible damage on one side of the building is reputed to be the result of over enthusiastic and not very skilful musket practice but may date from 1643 when a troop of Royalist cavalry were captured here.

South of the village a footpath off the road to Coxbench circumvents old quarry workings where the decaying remains of 12th century Horeston Castle stand on a prominent finger of sandstone.

Send a postcard from Horsley, if only to use the singular stone pillar-box on Church Street. Definitely not regulation issue but this local bit of community do-it-yourself has been in use since Christmas Eve 1894.

IBLE

North of the Via Gellia, a narrow ribbon of road loops up the north side of the valley into Ible with its thin dusting of farms and cottages. D. H. Lawrence stayed in this quiet and isolated spot for a time and set a short story, *Wintry Peacock*, here. Beside the road is a row of spring-fed stone water troughs. Referred to locally as the 'Twelve Apostles', these were once the main water supply for people and livestock in the village. The nearby house was formerly a Methodist chapel and probably dates from much later than the troughs but it would be nice to think the motivation for the troughs was perhaps a charitable act that also could serve as a religious advertisement. To give thanks and be appropriately reminded of the need to satisfy a more spiritual thirst.

A footpath leads beside The Beeches Farm and heads downhill to join the Via Gellia. Near the bottom of this track, all but lost in the scrubby undergrowth, is the ruin of Lode Mill. Built around 1700 it had a breastshot wheel driven by water from a dam further along the hillside. Part of the mill mechanism can still be seen inside the tumbledown building.

IDRIDGEHAY

'Ithersee' as it is often familiarly called, is one of a scatter of villages sharing the Ecclesbourne Valley along which runs a disused railway line and the Duffield to Wirksworth road. In South Sitch House it has a most interesting and remarkable timber-framed dwelling and one of the finest in the county. No household name noble owners or famous connections but locked up in its fabric the story of a landmark shift in living styles and social customs from medieval to modern.

A date stone of 1641 is generally believed to refer to a remodelling of a much earlier, single-storey aisled hall. This chimes exactly with early 17th century fashions. Before Elizabeth I, houses of any substance were built around a single large open hall with a central fire. A chimney now shows the position of the original fireplace at South Sitch but at that time smoke would probably have been left to find its own way out through the rafters — an arrangement that was generally thought to help toughen and preserve the exposed timbers. Private rooms, or solars, leading off the hall tended to be small and were very much subsidiary to the communal hub of the household. But domestic habits were changing and improved building techniques made it possible to respond. Household functions, such as cooking, were becoming more systematically organised and kept separate from living quarters. Individuals demanded more privacy. This meant bigger and better private chambers. The communal hall where once everyone gathered to socialise, eat and be entertained was reduced to a mere entrance area. Upper storeys were added. South Sitch probably witnessed this sea change in popular taste and is a rare survivor of the transition.

ILKESTON

Ilkeston is a town firmly rooted in an industrial past. Since the 18th century it has been associated with hosiery, coal and iron. The large open market area at the hub of the town is dotted with cast iron street lamps, pot-bellied iron troughs and a pit waggon filled with flowers, all decked out in the smart maroon and gold livery of Erewash Borough Council. Bennerley Viaduct is an important part of the legacy of Ilkeston's industrial past, but tucked away at the north-eastern fringe of the town it is often overlooked.

As if building a railway viaduct was not enough of a challenge, when the Great Northern Railway Company reached the Erewash Valley they also had to contend with land riddled by underground mine shafts and liable to subsidence. Their response was a unique run of latticed ironwork suspended on steel towers. Strong enough to take a twin track with load bearing well dispersed and sufficient tensile flexibility to withstand ground movement. Over a quarter of a mile long, the viaduct took three years to build, opening in 1878. It finally closed in 1973, though the last regular service train crossed in 1968. Now Bennerley stands in quiet retirement, a tribute to the designers and engineers of the pioneering early days of steam.

KING'S NEWTON

Not many people know that this pretty village in the south of the county gave its name to a variety of apple. Samuel Taylor, mine host of the Hardinge Arms in the 19th century, nurtured an accidental seedling he found growing in the roof thatch. He tended and grafted on his chance sapling until the product was bought out by a commercial grower who marketed the 'Newton Wonder' so successfully that it was soon a staple variety found in every self-respecting Victorian orchard. Taylor's original tree cropped until the 1940s before finally surrendering to the inevitabilities of old age and ending its days sending smoke drifting back up the chimney towards its rooftop origins. Though by that time the thatched roof of the tavern had been removed and replaced.

In Jawbone Lane, King's Newton the tradition of displaying a whale's jawbone has been maintained. An unusual sight anywhere but especially in a landlocked county.

KNOWLE HILL

If it is seclusion you hanker for, Knowle Hill house is the place. It is buried in the south Derbyshire countryside between the tiny hamlet of Ingleby, with its scatter of individual houses, a couple of farms and a pub that brews its own beer, and the village of Ticknall. There is no road access to Knowle Hill, only a private track and a public footpath. From the footpath the long, low brick building looks unremarkable. In the same way that most of an iceberg is hidden beneath the surface, what is visible is only the tip.

Walter Burdett, the third son of Derbyshire squire Sir Francis Burdett of nearby Foremark Hall, built the first house here in 1696. Walter was unmarried, 50 years of age and a moderately successful lawyer with chambers in London's Inner Temple. When his elder brother inherited the family home he decided to retire and chose Knowle Hill, adjacent to the Foremark estate, to build his home. The site is delightful — a steep hidden valley with a rippling stream. Not perhaps the most promising for building but without doubt the stuff of which dreams are made. Walter clearly needed both vision and ingenuity to turn his dream into reality.

Despite choosing to live in this quiet, away from it all spot, Walter was no recluse. At his 'bachelor pad' he hosted dinner parties at which the cream of south Derbyshire society gathered. All the local gentry — the Stanhopes from Bretby; the Curzons from Kedleston; the Harpurs from Calke; the Hardinges from King's Newton; the Cokes from Melbourne — were regular guests, enchanted by the house and its setting. Along the slopes of the valley, gardens were laid out in classical Italian style with statues set in niches, an avenue of limes, a cascade and walks. Knowle Hill remained largely unchanged until 1767, when Sir Robert Burdett, the 4th Baronet and Walter's great nephew, remodelled it.

Below and behind the single-storey cottage frontage of five rooms the house clambers down the side of the ravine on terraced revetments finally burrowing into the bedrock itself. Immediately below the top level is a courtyard with service buildings. Of these, stables and a coach house survive, but other outbuildings in the range that may have served as brewhouse or laundry have disappeared. In a corner of the yard is a circular summer house or luncheon room built in brick with mock battlements, gothic ogee windows and inside a decorative plaster frieze. From here a staircase leads down to a wine cellar and beyond to a grotto with 'secret' chambers. Clandestine meeting places and secret societies became a fashionable diversion during the 18th century. Sir Francis Dashwood, who for a time served as Chancellor of the Exchequer, presided over his infamous Hell-Fire Club from similar cave premises at West Wycombe in Buckinghamshire. Although a contemporary of Dashwood, there is no suggestion that Sir Robert Burdett was a member of this dissolute coterie or that anything as profane or scandalous as Dashwood was accused of indulging in took place at Knowle Hill. Most likely it was just an excitingly different place to entertain, and possibly gamble, with friends.

Although it became part of the Foremark estate, this remarkable house was largely neglected after Sir Robert's death. It served as a gamekeeper's cottage and was then rented to various tenants. By the time the last of these left, in the 1950s, the estate had been sold. When Knowle Hill was rescued by the Landmark Trust in 1995 many would have judged it beyond hope. Nature has reclaimed the garden but against all the odds the house has been restored and now enjoys a new lease of life as a unique holiday let.

LONGFORD

——— An external platform sheltered beneath projecting eaves gives a long, low wooden building the appearance of a railway station. In fact this is the site of the first cheese factory in England. The 'platform' was to make loading and unloading horse-drawn waggons easier. The benefits of pooling resources attracted local dairy farmers to set up their cheese making operation. An American, already living in England, Cornelius Schermerhorn, was employed as manager and production began in May 1870. As a co-operative venture it set a pattern that was immediately followed close by at Brailsford and Egginton as well as elsewhere in the county at Grangemill and Hartington. Of these, only Hartington, famous for its rich, blue-veined Stilton, is still actively producing cheese.

The former cheese factory at Longford.

Opposite the old cheese factory where two streams, Sutton Brook and Shirley Brook, meet there is an imposing former corn mill with a tiled roof, leaded windows and mellow brickwork. It was built in 1837 and animal feed was still being ground here on four pairs of millstones until the 1950s. The waterwheel and its housing are no longer in place but a lovely mill pond remains behind the building, the race running over a sluice-controlled weir at the point where the wheelhouse once stood. An overflow stream on the other side combined with the brooks almost turns the site into a mini-island. A prominent feature on the roof is the lucam, a cabin-like attic structure that contained the equipment for hoisting sacks of grain.

Cheese factory and mill buildings are both now private houses — part of the mix of old and new properties that make up this tiny village set just off Long Lane, a route laid by the Romans from Derventio, the garrison at Little Chester and now part of Derby, to Rocester in Staffordshire. The oldest building is St Chad's church. This dates from around 1400 and stands well outside the village in parkland next to Longford Hall. St Chad's has monuments to the Longford and Coke families who were past occupants of the hall. Fire necessitated significant reconstruction of Longford Hall but it retains lots of Tudor and Georgian features. One of the outbuildings is ventilated by a pattern of gaps in the brickwork. The spaces left form a series of diamond shapes and also spell out 'WC 1760'. In Sepycoe Lane, the gable of the former smithy has a similar design picked out in blue brick saying 'EC 1866'. Who the copycat was or whether the 'C' indicates a family bricklaying trademark is one of life's little mysteries.

LUMSDALE

Improved roads, a canal system and the rail network all ushered in as part and parcel of the industrial age made some previously isolated places accessible. Other areas were sidestepped into obscurity.

The narrow road that plunges into Lumsdale, near Matlock, is so steep and pinched it is hard to believe this forgotten valley was ever thought suitable for industrial development. It had one priceless asset — Bentley Brook. Water mills rely on a steady flow of water. Full-grown rivers are often too difficult to control and slow moving except at natural 'knickpoints'. Before the damming of its upper valley took place, the Derwent was particularly prone to flooding. Streams such as the Bonsall Brook at Cromford, chosen by Arkwright for his pioneering cotton spinning mill, and Bentley Brook, its flow concentrated by descent into the valley at Lumsdale, are ideal driving forces.

Lumsdale is best visited on foot starting from Upper Lumsdale. There are interesting walks on the higher ground towards Tansley, where bracken and tall spruce now cloak old quarrying activity. But follow the brook as closely as possible by lane and footpath to visit six ruined mills, the stone ribs and masonry skeletons peeping from undergrowth. The mills almost in the chronological order in which they were built, succeed one another nose to tail, each mill feeding in turn on the water expelled from upstream operations. The oldest and smallest probably dates from the 1500s. The last and largest, a cotton spinning mill, from the end of the 18th century. Bone for fertiliser, lead ore, minerals for paint manufacture and grain have all been ground between the millstones that turned in this valley. Cotton spinning continued into the 20th century.

Although some traces of dams and the small reservoirs remain most of the mill ponds disappeared as the wheels ceased to turn. The Arkwright Society has restored a pond by Lumsdale Farm to show how a series of pools and sluices created the interconnecting energy source down the valley. Outside the ruins of the mill immediately below the farm is a circular trough that was used for bleaching yarn. Material would have been suspended in bleaching agent from a wooden pole. A notch in the rim of the vat indicates where this rod slotted. A tall chimney in trees opposite the tumbledown remains of the mill marks the site of a former boilerhouse flue where gases were vented.

Technical ingenuity may have turned Lumsdale with its natural water resources into a pioneering industrial estate but it could not surmount the difficulties of access that came with its location. One by one, the mills closed but their fascinating legacy remains.

LUTUDARUM

—— Where is — or rather where was — Lutudarum? It is one of Derbyshire's biggest secrets. Not so much hidden as lost without trace and waiting to be found.

Although local contractors were licensed to dig and smelt ore, often taking advantage of slave labour, the Romans enforced a monopoly on lead throughout their empire. It was a valuable commodity. Refined lead ore, known as 'galena', yields small quantities of silver as well as lead. Much of what was produced in this country found its way directly to Rome.

One of the main centres in Derbyshire was Lutudarum. Over twenty Roman pigs have turned up at various sites in Derbyshire, all clearly marked as coming from the lead and silver works of the socii Lutudarenses or Lutudarum partnership, sometimes with Lutudarum abbreviated as LVT. One pig was unearthed near Brough on Humber, the port of exit for these early exports. The ingots were called 'pigs' because the molten metal was run off from the simple furnace along a channel with ingot moulds laid out on either side reminiscent of piglets suckling a sow.

Pigs of lead from Roman smelting operations have been found at Middleton, near Wirksworth (a leading contender for the site of Lutudarum), and in the churchyard at Cromford. In 1975, two ingots were unearthed in a field not far from the road just south of the village of Yeaveley. The assumption has been they were lost in transit — not easy considering the weight of these 'porkers' — either from the Middleton area or, if Lutudarum was further south, a site somewhere around Carsington. Construction work for Carsington Reservoir uncovered evidence of continual activity in the area spanning all four centuries of the Roman occupation, a finding significant in promoting Carsington as the current favourite location for Lutudarum. If true, this may also mean the site is now submerged below the waters of the reservoir.

One day perhaps the mystery will be solved. In the meantime we can let our fancy roam. Maybe Lutudarum appears once every hundred years like Brigadoon. If so, it is simply a matter of being in the right place at the right time.

MARKLAND GRIPS

—— Markland Grips is an attractive narrow gorge between Clowne and Elmton. Neolithic cave burials dating back to before 2000 BC have been discovered in the natural caverns that punctuate the valley sides. At the northern end of the valley, where Markland Grips and Hollinhill Grips meet, is a promontory fort. Triple earthwork ramparts with ditches enclose a triangular area of approximately 12 acres. Excavations on this splendid defensive position have shown it was occupied over a long period, from the Iron Age through to Roman times and beyond. The Archaeological Way footpath crosses the valley here on the line of a dismantled railway track and gives good views of the fort site and along the gorge.

MATLOCK

—— The county offices, high on steep Bank Road, are the administrative centre for Derbyshire. From 1893 to 1927, tramcars regularly climbed Bank Hill's 1 in 5½ gradient that made it the world's steepest tramway system. This operated from a decorative terminus shelter, that has now been transferred into Hall Leys Park, to a depot at the top of Bank Road. An engine house nearby at the junction of Rutland Street and Wellington Street can still be seen.

Derbyshire County Council occupies what was once a 'Hydro' — a hotel where guests took a variety of water treatments for their health — built to his own design by local textile tycoon John Smedley. Smedley was also responsible for Riber Castle, the brooding ruin, now housing a zoo, whose silhouette haunts Matlock's skyline. Riber stands on such an exposed and windswept site that it was built without a front door.

Unassuming Burton House, at 135 Smedley Street behind the county offices, is easily passed without a glance. Behind its rather ordinary exterior lies an interesting tale of covert wartime operations. This house was part of a secret emergency resistance set up to combat any invasion by German forces, codenamed 'Operation Sea Lion' and actively expected by the government

Matlock's former tram terminus shelter, now in Hall Leys Park.

authorities in the weeks following the evacuation of Dunkirk. On the surface, 135 Smedley Street in 1940 was nothing more than the simple tailor's shop it appeared to be. Beneath the façade of unexceptional ordinariness that was such an essential part of its cover, this house doubled as Ground Station Zero TX, a communications and intelligence command centre manned by specially trained volunteers. Fortunately, the anticipated invasion did not take place and 135 Smedley Street, after its exciting and clandestine interlude, was allowed to return to normal.

MATLOCK BATH

――――― At one time there were seven 'Matlocks'. Apart from Matlock Bath, which has retained a separate identity, the others including Matlock Bridge, Matlock Green and Matlock Bank are now pretty much subsumed into a single Matlock Town identity. The thermal spring that added the distinction 'Bath' to this particular Matlock still runs through a grotto in Temple Road car park. 'Thermal' is a relative term here and at 68° Fahrenheit, Matlock's waters were some 20° colder than those of market leaders and rivals, Bath and Buxton. The Temple Road grotto marks the site of the first bath house, built here in 1698. As a spa Matlock Bath was a slow starter but gradually business grew and two more baths were added during the course of the next century.

By the time the railway reached Matlock Bath in 1848, enabling the development from spa to more of an all round resort with a wide range of visitor attractions, Lovers' Walks were already popular, well-established pleasure gardens. The lower route follows the riverside while a second path climbs up through lush woodland to give fine views. Most people enjoy the scenery and appreciate the trees and wild flowers in a general sense but there is a treasure here few recognise. The wild service tree is a rare native species related to the whitebeam and the rowan. It thrives in old, undisturbed woodland, enjoys the taste of limestone beneath its roots and can grow up to a height of 60 feet. Its leaves are lobed with a serrated edge. The furrowed bark develops a characteristic square pattern leading to the nickname 'chequer tree'. Small brown fruits hanging in clusters appear in the autumn and follow a flush of delicate white flower blossom. Hard, bitter flesh is miraculously transformed when the berries are exposed to frost. This converts the sugars in the fruit, a process known as 'bletting'.

In past times the bletted fruits of the wild service tree were collected and eaten as titbits, much like sweets. Seeds have been found in prehistoric middens or waste pits, showing that our ancestors were no different from us in enjoying a tasty treat. Beer was also brewed using the berries, offering one of a number of possible explanations for the continuous use of a chequerboard as a tavern sign from ancient Egypt in the time of the Pharaohs through to the numerous 'Chequers' public houses familiar today.

Looking is fine but not picking. Please remember the Countryside Code and the need to protect wildlife, plants and trees. The woodland of Lovers' Walks is designated as a Site of Special Scientific Interest (SSSI).

❧ MEERBROOK SOUGH

—— As large scale commercial lead mining began to take over from the operations of individual miners, ever deeper seams of ore were exploited and planned drainage became essential. Soughs, or underground channels, were dug to carry floodwater away from the mineshafts.

The first soughs discharging water into the Derwent Valley were most probably planned by Cornelius Vermuyden, who arrived in the county in 1629 having cut his teeth draining the Dutch dykes, reclaiming sections of Fenland in East Anglia, and working on flood prevention schemes for the river Thames. He quickly went 'native' in Derbyshire, acquiring local lead mining rights and eventually becoming Barmaster of the ancient lead miners' court.

How many soughs were driven before steam engines took over the task of emptying the deep mines of floodwater during the 19th century is anybody's guess. There are at least six major channels beneath Wirksworth and probably hundreds in all. Excavating the sough tunnels was a hard and dangerous occupation. Diggers worked by candlelight using hand tools and gunpowder that they were invariably expected to provide for themselves. Pay averaged one shilling a day for diggers and pumpmen in the 18th century, while the really unpleasant job of periodically cleaning out accumulated mud and sludge to allow the miners to work, paid up to double that amount.

Meerbrook Sough, 2½ miles in length with a further 2½ miles of tributaries, was one of the business enterprises of the industrialist Francis Hurt of Alderwasley. Unseen beside waterworks off the A6, a couple of miles south of Cromford, the tailrace of Meerbrook Sough can still be seen, depositing 1,000s of gallons of water each day into the river Derwent. Cutting the soughs drained the mines but by altering the water table caused problems elsewhere. Sir Richard Arkwright closed two mills because water used to power cotton spinning machinery dried up when Meerbrook was dug. There must have been some uncomfortable domestic confrontations because Francis Hurt's son had married Richard Arkwright's daughter. Difficulties were also caused for the Cromford Canal whose water supply was sufficiently undercut by an expanded Meerbrook Sough to necessitate building a pumphouse at Leawood, half a mile upriver on the opposite bank to that on which Meerbrook Sough emerges. The beam engine housed inside was capable of pumping 31 tons of water per minute to ensure the water level required in the canal. It has been restored and is occasionally fired up for visitors.

MELBOURNE

A stroll around Melbourne is full of delightful surprises. There are lots of back roads and side streets to explore, all with intriguing brick or stone properties including a cruck-framed (see Osmaston entry) thatched cottage just up the hill from the market place. Then there is Melbourne Hall, once the rectory, and the magnificent church of St Michael and St Mary next door. Why all this grandeur in what is essentially a rural backwater? The answer is that the first Bishop of Carlisle was granted ownership by Henry I. His eminence desperately needed a getaway; a quiet retreat and place of refuge far removed from the lawlessness and tribulations of life in his wild, border diocese. The Church held on to extensive land and property here until the 17th century, by which time life on the Scottish borders had become easier.

The church and hall overshadow some smaller surrounding buildings that although less obviously grand are worthy of attention. To the west of the church is a fine tithe barn. From the end of the 8th century the church was entitled to one tenth of the produce of the parish and great barns like these were built to store its share of the grain harvest. Next to the vicarage an old stone property marks the site where, in 1707, the master ironsmith Robert Bakewell set up his forge to complete a series of commissions at the hall. One of the finest examples of Bakewell's workmanship to be found anywhere stands in the hall grounds (open Wednesday and weekend afternoons from spring through to autumn); a unique gilded cage arbour in wrought iron decorated in intricate detail.

A cruck-framed cottage in Melbourne.

MIDDLETON BY YOULGREAVE

▬▬ This ancient, lived in, unspoiled rural hamlet has two notable memorials. A discreet plaque in the village centre remembers six young men, the crew of a Wellington bomber, RAF number BJ652, who lost their lives in a crash less than a mile away in 1944. Behind the former Congregational chapel in a field surrounded by railings is the tomb of Thomas Bateman, a famous 19th century Derbyshire archaeologist and antiquarian. Bateman dug barrows and other ancient sites at a prodigious rate, often more than one a day, but he still managed to be more meticulous with his finds than many of his contemporaries.

A wide rock and rubble path descends between a cluster of cottages and farmhouses. This leads down through steep cliffs and tall trees. Heavy shade contributes to a habitat that is perfect for encrusting lichens and hart's-tongue. At the foot is beautiful Bradford Dale, a signature Derbyshire dale where shallow clear waters course through a steep, wooded limestone valley and dippers nest in the banks.

Where the path meets the dale there is a flat area. A cold bright spring emerges from the foot of a cliff just a few yards upstream and ponds have been created. Stone walls here form small, triangular enclosures through which the waters run. These were once used as holding pens where sheep waited to have excess dirt and grease washed from their fleeces before shearing. Sheep are good swimmers but can become waterlogged and the washing process was closely controlled. Clean wool weighs less but commanded a higher price and made the effort of washing the animals worthwhile. Hidden in undergrowth lie the ruins of a pumping station. Until the 1930s this tapped water from a spring and pumped it up to the village where the old well head still declares 'The Lord's Gift 1876'.

Sir Christopher Fullwood was discovered hiding in Bradford Dale after fleeing the Parliamentarian forces that were about to overrun his home in the village, Fullwood Hall. Sir Christopher was shot and captured. His wounds proved fatal and Fullwood Hall was completely destroyed but the site, in the field by Castle Farm opposite the Congregational chapel, is still referred to as 'Fullwood's Castle'.

🌿 MILFORD

—— How do you survey a railway or a road to ensure an exact line is followed? Or guarantee a tunnel started at both ends simultaneously meets in the middle? Nowadays, of course, we have accurate maps and the pinpoint precision of ground positioning satellites. Before the advent of such 'hi-tech' aids methods had hardly changed from Roman times. First of all routes were investigated on foot and by horseback. Surveying was done by eye from horizon to horizon, compass bearings taken and angles plotted on charts. Many of the critical sighting points were of a temporary nature and no longer survive. High on Chevin Hill a rather plain looking square brick tower used by George Stephenson during 1839 and 1840 to align Milford tunnel, part of the Derby to Sheffield railway, still stands. The tower originally had four storeys and was probably built so substantially in order to house drilling equipment used to cut the air shafts that can also be seen emerging on the ridge following the line of the track below.

The accuracy of the railway pioneers is astonishing. Over a long route, the slightest inaccuracy at the start would compound over the miles yet the tracks are unerring. No last minute dog-legs to hit their destination.

Stephenson, of course, made his home in Derbyshire and is buried in front of the altar at Holy Trinity church, Chesterfield. The sighting tower at Milford represents a more unusual memorial to his skill.

MONK'S DALE

I really should not tell you about Monk's Dale. This undeveloped hidden valley is one of Derbyshire's best kept secrets. The dale is about 1½ miles long and runs northwards from the Wye Valley cutting between Wormhill and Tideswell. In the height of summer Lathkill Dale, with its improved access and information points, may receive as many as 1,000 visitors per day, Dovedale two or three times that number. At Monk's Dale the number may be down to single figures.

The Limestone Way long distance footpath sidesteps Monk's Dale to pick up its route north of the dale along a linking chain of small, pretty limestone valleys: Peter Dale, Hay Dale and Dam Dale. But there is a footpath through Monk's Dale, following the rough floor of the watercourse between the slopes on which ash and sycamore grow. It can be a wet scramble in places. Look out for build-ups of tufa, a porous calcium carbonate deposit with a pitted surface that was once popular in rock gardens, in the bed of the stream. Please keep to the path. Access is not permitted to the land on either side. Preserving the unspoiled natural state of the dale requires extreme care and sensitivity from visitors.

The environment sometimes needs a helping hand and Monk's Dale is sensitively managed by English Nature to preserve a typical limestone dale habitat. Overall, their approach is minimalist with controlled grazing and some coppicing to encourage a mix of flora and fauna that appreciate the cycle of opening up woodland followed by gradual regrowth.

According to an intriguing legend there is a secret tunnel leading to the dale from Tideswell. If not exactly likely, it is not impossible for either a man-made, or natural, underground cave to exist. The wider, southern entrance was formed in the geological past by volcanic action.

MONYASH

—— A number of lanes and footpaths meet at Monyash, a legacy of its former significance as a lead mining centre and, in the Middle Ages, as a cattle market. Farmhouses with their adjacent pens, barns and yards in the village give it a distinct rural feel. A market cross stands on the small green. Fere Mere, the pretty village pond, is fed by an underground spring. It once supplied the village's domestic water and is surrounded by a low protective stone wall to keep passing livestock out. Monyash stands at the head of scenic Lathkill Dale where a combination of relatively easy walking and hard to rival beauty attracts lots of visitors.

The crystal clear waters of the upper Lathkill are unpredictable, responding to seasonal weather conditions. Sometimes emerging in a torrent from Lathkill Head Cave, sometimes seeping almost imperceptibly through the riverbed further down the valley. Dippers can be spotted downstream, flying low over the river or perched on rocks. These plump-breasted birds with their distinctive white bib and characteristic bobbing action disappear under the water to search the riverbed for food. Rare plants such as Jacob's Ladder, gold-dusted stamens springing from its rich blue flowers, and Yellow Rattle can be found. In the spring, swathes of Early Purple Orchid mantle the slopes and there are traces of mills and mines. It has to be seen. But for solitude, look elsewhere. Like Cales Dale for instance. Reached by a footbridge that uses a wooden extension linked to the stone remains of an earlier, now ruined, bridge to cross the river Lathkill, a mile below Monyash.

Cales Dale has steep sides crowned with limestone outcrops. Scrub hawthorn and ash spread up the slopes. The dale has its own capricious tributary stream that in the right conditions spouts in a cataract from a fissure in the limestone. Higher up the dale are caves but before that point a scramble up a rocky incline leads to One Ash Grange. Here the Limestone Way cuts through the farmyard and heads west back towards Monyash village. There was a settlement at One Ash in Saxon times. Now it is just a single farmhouse with extensive outbuildings on the site of a 12th century medieval grange that belonged to the Cistercian monks of Roche Abbey, near Maltby in Yorkshire. As an order the Cistercians deliberately sought out the most isolated locations. It was mainly lay brothers who tended the hornless Old Limestone sheep on the surrounding hills, but even lay brethren were required to attend prayers sessions twice a day and to lead a life of austerity. The remoteness of One Ash also made it a useful place of banishment for any monk found guilty of misbehaviour at the mother house.

Sheep were kept predominantly for wool in the Middle Ages. Look out for 'creep holes', tunnel-like gaps built into the drystone walls, that allow sheep to wander from field to field but are small enough to prevent cattle straying. The smaller the creep hole, the older it is likely to be. Modern sheep tend to be much larger than the breeds the monks would have been used to keeping.

Do not miss the row of stone pigsties in the farmyard. These are probably 19th century additions to the farm that gradually fell into disuse as increasingly intensive farming methods made them unprofitable. Unlike sheep, pigs are not well equipped for living in these upland conditions. By nature and inclination they are creatures of the woodland. They feel the cold, burn in the sun, and need protection from the elements. These 'pen and run' sties with a small shelter and exercise yard are typical of those that became popular from the middle of the 18th century and through Victorian times. Each sty is designed for two pigs or a sow with a litter. Pigs are not fussy eaters and were commonly fed on scraps from the kitchen or on dairy waste.

Amongst the jumble of redundant buildings at One Ash is a vaulted stone chamber cut back into the rock. Stone slabs at the rear indicate this was probably a cold store for food. There is also an uncomfortable looking tandem 'privy' proving, should there be any doubt, that medieval sanitation on the farm was, to say the least, fairly basic.

MORLEY

Turn off the A608 heading north-east from Derby and the countryside changes abruptly. Drystone walls, narrow lanes and deeply folded hills have a much more rural character. Morley is off the beaten track but informed visitors, some following the Midshires Way footpath, will notice St Matthew's church with its acclaimed Norman architecture complemented by early stained glass and medieval tiles rescued from the ruins of Dale Abbey following the Reformation. It is worth exploring just a little further.

In the churchyard is an ancient gateway, one of the fragments left of old Morley Hall. This was the home of the former Lords of the Manor of Morley. Before it was demolished, in the latter half of the 18th century, the hall stood in the field beside the church. Parish records show that John Stathum, Lord of the Manor in the early 15th century, gave bread to the poor. He may well have carried out his charitable deed at this churchyard gate because it is still referred to locally as 'loaf gate'. Some outbuildings dating from the time of the hall survived demolition including an old tithe barn behind the church, now a private house. But we may never know if the story of a secret passage linking church and hall is fact or fiction.

🌿 MORLEY MOOR

——— The names of Brick Kiln Road and Quarry Road are giveaways to former activity on Morley Moor. At one time the local stone was much in demand for making grindstones and as sharpening stones for agricultural implements. Now the quarries are closed and silent and the site of former brickworking is a nature reserve. Almshouses Lane is also self-explanatory. An attractive row of six almshouses, now with some more recently built modern residences for company, was the gift of the Sacheverell family, Lords of the Manor in the 17th century. From here it is a ten minute walk across the moor to Morley church following the prehistoric route known by its Anglo-Saxon name as the 'Portway'.

About halfway is the enigmatic Morley mound, approximately 7 yards high and 22 yards wide at the base with the faint remains of an encircling moat. The mound is overgrown by trees but tapers to a small flat platform at the summit. What it was for has puzzled historians for centuries. Currently the smart money is on it being an advance lookout point for Horeston Castle 1½ miles away. Other suggestions include a motte and bailey castle (surely too small), a Roman survey point for laying out Ryknield Street (but this runs half a mile away) or a local meeting place. The Domesday Book records a meeting place known as the 'Morlestone' in 1086. A definite possibility but a much less significant mound closer to the church is an alternative contender as a site for communal gatherings. What confuses the issue is that the Portway goes around the mound suggesting the earthwork could be much older than anyone thinks. When in doubt, archaeologists usually fall back on 'ceremonial' or 'ritual' as an explanation. This time they may be right.

🌿 MUGGINTON

——— A memorial pays tribute to the crew of a World War II bomber that crash-landed here. All Saints' church contains an earlier memorial. An altar-tomb in the Kniveton chapel is decorated with detailed brass portraits of the finest quality, depicting Sir Nicholas Kniveton and his wife Joanna. In true medieval knightly style, Sir Nicholas is shown with his faithful hunting hound at his feet.

Mugginton was once at the heart of Duffield Frith, a major royal hunting forest. The Frith was big business as well as a playground in the Middle Ages with hunting rights, pasture and pannage (the right to graze swine), and timber all bringing in the profits. Forests were divided into administrative wards, each holding their own court to deal with cases of trespass, poaching and other infringements, and into separate parks where open space and woodland were managed to provide ideal hunting conditions. It all vanished with the enclosures and felling that took place in the 17th century but echoes remain in old names and in landscape features. Across the area there are numerous farms and place names with 'park' attached. Between Duffield and Milford is a 'Courthouse' Farm.

A footpath skirting the northern boundary of the area still known as Ravensdale Park, just outside Mugginton, follows for part of its route the line of the medieval park pale. This earthwork consisting of a bank and ditch would originally have been topped with oak palings or a thick thorny hedge to make a deerproof fence. Any palings have long since vanished and the earthen bank has become much less conspicuous but for stretches of its length traces survive and can be clearly seen.

NEW MILLS

The original 'new' mill was Berde Mill, a 13th century corn mill. It became New Mills, plural, in 1775. The population grew swiftly with industrialisation and the town of New Mills was officially formed in 1884 when a collection of scattered hamlets: Beard, Ollersett, Thornsett and Whitle joined with Newtown. The high promontory of Torr Top, in the centre of New Mills, is surrounded on three sides by water; the river Sett flowing south down the eastern flank where it joins the river Goyt flowing first westerly and then meandering northwards through a deep sandstone ravine sculpted over 15,000 years ago by retreating glacial meltwater.

Building stone, water for power and the natural rock terraces of the Torrs Gorge provided an ideal combination of resources that were exploited to the full by the cotton barons of Industrial Revolution England. In the sense that it simply deserves to be far more widely known, the whole of New Mills with its combination of spectacular setting, beautiful countryside and industrial heritage, is hidden. But for those who make the effort, the Heritage and Information Centre, at the top of cobbled Rock Mill Lane overlooking the gorge, has a wealth of material and displays on the background and key sites.

Among the less publicised places to visit is Newtown Marina. Although modernised, this former basin on the Peak Forest Canal has the remains of a wooden jib crane and of stone stables. Teams of draught horses once hauled narrow boats from the canal terminus at nearby Buxworth Basin to Marple in Cheshire and worked the tramway connecting Buxworth to the limestone quarries. Opposite the marina, a long, single-storey building converted to industrial units is the only remaining ropewalk building in New Mills. Rope was in demand in the local collieries and mills as well as on the canals. The shape of the building is typical of the traditional method of manufacture that used devices known as 'travellers' moving slowly along a rail, first twisting the hemp fibres and then weaving the strands into thick rope.

NEWTON SOLNEY

—— Even in the days when rank and wealth was accompanied by privilege, thumbing your nose at public opinion was still a risky business. Position and status came with responsibility and expectations about socially acceptable behaviour. Nobody likes a show off. In 1795, Abraham Hoskins, a successful solicitor from Burton upon Trent in Staffordshire, whose family had made money from a brick making business in Newton Solney, purchased the local manor and estates and set about creating a lifestyle to match his Lord of the Manor ambitions. Sir Jeffrey Wyatville, a top architect of the day, was commissioned to design a fine new house befitting Hoskins' rising status. Wyatville produced plans for an impressive hall to be set in landscaped parkland on the edge of Newton Solney village. It was not this building which caused a problem but a frivolous addition half a mile away.

In the 18th and 19th centuries there was a fashion for elaborate architectural follies. Practical jokes in stone, brick and mortar — Greek temples, Roman arches, Chinese pagodas and strikingly conceived towers began to appear in the parks of the great houses. Hoskins' 'folly' was Bladon Castle. Built along the summit of Bladon Hill, it consisted of a long, high brick wall, decorated with battlements, dominating the skyline overlooking Newton Solney and the Trent Valley. From a distance it had the appearance of the genuine article but was in fact mere frontage, an effect rather like a modern film set.

Designed to impress, the 'castle' certainly caused a stir. By common report, the local outcry was such that in order to take the heat out of the situation, Hoskins added a central block of rooms and two towers behind the wall and moved in, thereby at least giving the folly a practical purpose. It was to prove a 'double whammy'. The extra expense helped to put additional pressure on Hoskins' already stretched finances so that he was soon forced into selling his new house at Newton Solney. Also, because the site was never intended as a place to live, it lacked the basic necessity of water. In the absence of efficient pumps it meant supplies had to be hauled by mule some distance uphill.

Hoskins' star may have flared briefly but for that short time it blazed bright and left a lasting legacy. The grand house he built at Newton Solney is now a hotel. Bladon Castle is in private hands and, as if still wary of public disapproval, it is all but veiled from public view by Castle Wood which has grown up thickly on all sides to guard its privacy from the public road below.

OCKBROOK

——— It is a long way from Moravia to Derbyshire, but the United Brethren, popularly known as the Moravians, were zealous missionaries. Protestantism tends to begin its history with Martin Luther. The Moravians trace their origins back even earlier to the church set up in the middle of the 15th century in honour of the memory of John Hus, a martyred priest. Reinventing themselves in the early 1700s they began to attract converts and to spread their message more widely. Among the people they impressed with their missionary energy were a young John Wesley and a farmer from Ockbrook called Isaac Freeson.

In 1739, the same year that Wesley began the round of open-air preaching that planted the roots of Methodism, Freeson asked a Moravian evangelist to address a group of people in one of his farm outbuildings. A decade later the Moravians were invited back permanently. It was not a universally welcome move. Many locals were initially suspicious of the newcomers but gradually people were won over. The settlement at Ockbrook, between Derby and Nottingham, became for many years the Moravians' headquarters in England.

As a community the Moravians were well organised and self-sufficient. The brethren farmed, brewed and made their own clothes. Individuals led relatively austere lives with strict rules governing the segregation of single men and women. A chapel of red brick was built but masonry recycled from the ruins of Dale Abbey is also incorporated in some of the properties. Many of the buildings are now of listed status and the whole site is a designated conservation area. The settlement changed as communal living went out of style but the formality of the Moravian approach is reflected in the simple elegance of the buildings, the open spaces and the compact orderliness of neat gardens.

Moravian Church Estates still own the site, although not all of the modern-day tenants are church members. The United Brethren are now a part of the wider Christian community in the local area.

OLD BRAMPTON

Old Brampton stretches along either side of one of a number of routes connecting the villages around Chesterfield with Baslow and the Derwent Valley over the eastern moors.

Between the village and neighbouring Cutthorpe, attractive woodland shelters the Linacre Reservoirs. Both Brampton Hall, near the medieval parish church, and Cutthorpe Hall, in fields along Green Lane south of the village, are historic old properties that share tales of secret underground passages.

West of Old Brampton and just outside the Peak District National Park boundary is the quaintly named Puddingpie Hill. It is said to get its culinary nickname from its resemblance to a steamed pudding in the times when limestone, carted here from across the moors, was regularly burned to produce lime for use on the local fields.

A local farmer, John Furniss, has left his imprint on Puddingpie Hill in the shape of a chair carved out of rock beside the road and inscribed: 'Sit ye down on chair by John Furniss of Moorhay Farm Wigley 1888'. It is not the only memorial left by the unconventional Farmer Furniss in that same year. Close by Moorhay Farm, large blocks of stone mark the spot where he buried his young wife Elizabeth, choosing to lay her to rest on the land they tended together rather than in the village churchyard as might be expected.

OSMASTON

—— There is precious little thatch to be found in Derbyshire but Osmaston, off the A52 between Derby and Ashbourne, does its best to make up. By the village pond, which has an unusual bench made entirely of horseshoes, is a fine example of a cruck-framed cottage. This deceptively simple building technique appeared in the 14th century. Unlike more common box-framing, where the weight of the roof is supported by resting beams on upright wall posts, the strength of the cruck-frame is independent of the walls. In fact, take the walls away and the structure remains solid. The A-shaped cruck is made from twin timbers, cut to match from a single naturally curving tree trunk and braced with a cross-tie. Oak is commonly used but some crucks are of black poplar, a tree that tends to grow at an angle and may have inspired the first cruck builder. Restricted width is the one real design drawback with a cruck-frame. It is unusual to find a building in which the bay between the timbers is more than 16 to 18 feet across, roughly the old English measurement of a perch. However, that was once a very practical size, generally reckoned to be the amount of space needed for four oxen abreast.

From the pond, a path leads away from the village along a lime-fringed avenue into Osmaston Park. In the grounds, which are enhanced by a string of attractive lakes, is a plant nursery with an astonishing tall, graceful square tower. It looks like a refugee that has slipped in from a Tuscan hill village. The man responsible is Francis Wright of the Butterley Company who built a manor house in the park during the 19th century. When plans were drawn up, the intention was to provide a single chimney to serve the entire manor house, into which all the individual fireplaces would feed. In the event it never worked efficiently but it did survive the demolition of the manor itself in the 1960s.

 ## OVER HADDON

——— Gold! In Derbyshire? In 1854, unconfirmed reports started feverish speculation and the Lathkill gold rush was underway. The Over Haddon Gold and Silver Company was formed and shares sold before the 'gold' was discovered to be of the fools' variety. It must have been fun while it lasted.

The village does have assets of a different kind. The captivating views from its rocky perch above Lathkill Dale are beyond price.

PADLEY

——— Annually, in July, a pilgrimage sets off along a track leading from Grindleford station to Padley chapel to commemorate the martyrdom of two Roman Catholic priests. Robert Ludlam and Nicholas Garlick were caught celebrating mass with the Fitzherberts of Padley Manor in 1588. Their gruesome end is described in the entry for Derby. The

Fitzherbert brothers, John and Thomas, escaped execution but failed to survive long in gaol, their deaths probably being a direct result of the squalid conditions they would have encountered. Padley Manor fell into disrepair but the gatehouse building that had housed the small private chapel survived. This was put to use as a barn, cow byre and workmen's shelter until finally rescued and restored in 1932. Incredibly, the table stone of the original altar was discovered on site. After a gap of 345 years mass was once again observed. The chapel building, a plain, gabled rectangle, is not particularly remarkable but inside can be seen parts of the original hammerbeam roof with ornamental angels. The use of projecting hammerbeams to support the weight of the roof adds height and space by removing the need for tie beams running the width of the building.

The annual pilgrimage to Padley is a well-publicised event that attracts a lot of visitors but few people take advantage of the opportunity to explore beyond the chapel. Nearby are the foundations of the old Fitzherbert manor, built in the middle of the 14th century on even older footings, with rooms arranged around a central courtyard. Where the great hall once stood are the remains of a central hearth. This would have been used for cooking as well as comfort, with smoke left to find its own way out between the exposed timbers of the roof. In medieval times life revolved around the hall. Important family members had their private chambers, and the base of a spiral staircase remains that would have led from the hall to rooms on two storeys. But these separate upper rooms, or solars, were small. Both the functional and social hub of the medieval aristocratic household was the communal hall.

Behind Padley chapel is the steep slope of Bole Hill. From here 1¼ million tons of gritstone were quarried to build Derwent Dam on the upper reaches of the river, 1,000 feet wide by 100 feet high. Trees have crept back to reclaim the slopes that lead up to higher ground with moorland beyond. Burbage Brook etches a deep gorge along the flank of Bole Hill on its way to the Derwent. In summer, a stroll through the older mixed woodland — alder by the brook, oak and silver birch further up the slopes — provides an opportunity to spot the elusive pied flycatcher. It was as recently as 1945 that a breeding pair was recorded in Padley Gorge, a first for England at the time. This small rare bird is a spring arrival, battling the elements to migrate from North Africa and the Mediterranean fringe to those areas of northern England and Wales with a profusion of oak and birch and where high rainfall can be expected. The male, black above and white below with white wing bars, is more distinctive than the brown and cream female but both are acrobatic flyers darting and turning in the air as they catch insects on the wing.

PARWICH

A network of narrow roads and back lanes wind around the jumble of mostly limestone cottages, the oldest of which have attractive mullion windows. Three-storey Parwich Hall built in the 18th century stands out from the crowd with its distinctive red-brick façade overlooking the limestone village. It is set on a slight elevation on the lower slopes of the hill that rising steeply to an altitude of almost 1,000 feet dominates the village.

Parwich's duck pond.

In many communities, village greens or 'common land' where free-ranging livestock could be herded for safety disappeared with the enclosure acts of the 18th and 19th centuries. Exceptionally, here at Parwich, a number of small greens survive and are dotted oasis-like in the village centre, the largest complete with stone-lined brook and duck pond.

PENTRICH

—— Why has Pentrich retained a degree of rural character lost by its near neighbours? The reason progress was effectively put on hold is that the village became the focus for England's last revolution. After 1817, Pentrich was never quite the same. It is a story famous locally but little heard further afield.

War with Napoleon generated a demand for iron and textile products that the mills and furnaces of Derbyshire, as elsewhere, were happy to supply. After victory at Waterloo, demand dropped, recession loomed and belts began to be tightened. 1816 was a bad year for the harvest. Workers' meetings were held in the industrial midlands and in the north of England. Mutterings about the need for reform were heard and revolution was in the air. The Government was rattled and determined to come down hard on any potential rebellion. When some men from Pentrich actually began a march the reaction of the authorities was swift and ruthless. Arrests were made and at the subsequent trial, three men received the death sentence, fourteen more were condemned to transportation and a further six jailed. Others who had managed to escape official notice lived in fear of being informed against. The houses of those arrested were demolished but the story of England's last rebellion can still be followed at sites around the village thanks to a 'Revolution Trail' created by Pentrich Historical Society. Discreet plaques sum up events at the place where they happened. Skip the aerobics class before you visit Pentrich and let the 50 steps that lead to St Matthew's church provide you with the necessary exercise.

Outside the village a grassy track leads northwards towards Coneygrey Farm. Hard to believe this is the great Roman Ryknield Street along which the legions marched from the Fosse

Way in the Cotswolds via Little Chester at Derby to join Ermine Street in Yorkshire. The route is well worn and clear as it leaves Pentrich but a mile further on, where it passes Coneygrey Farm, it becomes much less distinct. Castle Hill, in the field after the farm, bears the faint earthwork imprint of an early Roman fortlet; a small but important outpost guarding the road that would have followed the same pattern of drills, parades and patrols as in all Roman garrisons whether here in the valley of the river Amber or on the banks of the Nile. Raised banks can still be seen on a ridge to the right of the footpath and the occasional block of stone breaks through the surface of the turf. More roughly worked stone debris occurs on the hillside. It is a splendid vantage point with fine views across the Amber Valley to Wingfield Park and the ruins of Wingfield Manor.

This milestone can be seen at Pentrich Lane End.

PENTRICH LANE END

—— The Pentrich villagers took advantage of a strategic position between the two main routes northwards from Derby, one following the Derwent Valley to the west and the other the line of Roman Ryknield Street east of the village, to set up a turnpike on the connecting road. Money raised by charging travellers a toll for using the road through the village paid for its upkeep. By law, the Turnpike Trust had to erect a milestone and this can still be seen at Pentrich Lane End on the grass verge near the junction.

PILSBURY

—— Most people choose to explore the middle reaches of the river Dove, between Hartington and Thorpe. Here, Beresford Dale, Wolfscote Dale, Mill Dale and Dovedale lead one to another, each popular and outstandingly beautiful. Upstream, the Dove is comparatively neglected and unfairly so because it has its own special sights. One of these is Pilsbury Castle, 3 miles north of Hartington and widely acknowledged as the best preserved of all the motte and bailey sites in Derbyshire. There is little else here, just a couple of smoky grey farm buildings acting as counterpoint to this remote, enigmatic mound.

'Bury' in the name suggests there was a 'burh' or Saxon fortification here before the Normans redesigned the motte and built their castle around 1100. The position controls an important ford across the Dove and it is possible the origins of Pilsbury go back even further to the Iron Age or before. It is all supposition because there has been only limited excavation work carried out. In many ways that has helped to conserve the site and to preserve a romantic interest that allows all possibilities. Every archaeological dig, even the most sensitively handled, is in essence destructive. And it is good to leave a few mysteries to inspire the imagination.

PRIESTCLIFFE

—— Landscape change tends to come gradually. Occasionally events speed things up. A system of cultivation based on common ownership and shared grazing rights — of large open fields divided into unfenced furlong strips — came to an end with the gathering pace of enclosures during the 18th century. Traces remain of earlier ways in old field boundaries and in characteristic ridge and furrow ploughing patterns. 'Lynchets', terraces created by contour ploughing across hillsides, are the rarest signs of pre-enclosure farming. Quite when lynchets were formed is a matter of debate. They may date from Iron Age times or be as recent as Saxon. It is likely that some were in continuous cultivation over the whole of this span of time. This shows just how precious all land capable of growing crops was, even rough terrain, because ploughing across a slope with a team of yoked oxen must have been tough and demanding work. Successive tilling broadened the series of stepped banks as the action of the plough gradually moved soil further downhill. The high ground south of Miller's Dale is one of the best areas to search out lynchets. On Horse Stead, a hill south-east of the sparse scatter of houses that make up Priestcliffe, there are some fine examples that are particularly well defined in the shadows cast by a dipping sun in the late afternoon.

QUARNDON

—— On the outskirts of Derby, this modern village looks out over Kedleston Park. Kedleston Hall was built by Nathaniel Curzon, 1st Baron Scarsdale in 1760, latest in a succession of houses on the site since the family moved in early in the 12th century. The Curzons still live at the hall but the property is now owned by the National Trust and opens to visitors occasionally during the summer. The architect, Robert Adam, did some of his finest work at Kedleston, not just on the hall but also in the grounds, designing the Boathouse, North Lodge and the bridge spanning Cutler Brook.

Kedleston is the main attraction here but Quarndon itself is interesting. In the 19th century the Curzons had aspirations to turn Quarndon into a spa. The village well was fed by a mineral rich spring, its waters containing iron salts that oxidised on exposure to the air. An elaborate castellated façade was erected to make a feature of the well and water was bottled ready for sale. In the grounds of Kedleston a bath house was built to take advantage of a thermal spring. The final investment in this industrious exercise in diversification was a hotel for those tempted to 'take the waters'. Unfortunately, before the spa was even properly launched, a geological hiccup reduced the village well to a trickle without warning and doomed the entire enterprise. The Bath House still stands and can be seen on Kedleston Golf Course. The hotel served other purposes but is now once more a hotel. The village well still drips on occasions behind its impressive Gothic frontage, a meagre unnoticed spot of dribble from the mouth of a lion's head set low down in a side wall of the padlocked well chamber.

This elaborate façade fronts the village well at Quarndon.

🌿 REPTON

────── It is 7th century England, the Dark Ages, and King Penda has turned the family business started by his grandfather Crida, into the most powerful of the mini-kingdoms that jostle for power in the land. Repton in the Trent Valley is his capital...

The Mercian kings are said to have been crowned on the summit of Askew Hill, a few minutes pleasant climb east of the village. Penda's long rule straddled the transition from pagan beliefs to Christianity. The medieval cross at Repton probably marks the site where the message of the Gospels was first preached in Derbyshire and possibly first heard anywhere in the midlands. Penda claimed descent from Woden himself and kept faith with the gods of Scandinavian mythology. He lived and died by the sword and raised more than a little hell along the way. By the time of his death, in battle as a geriatric old man, he must surely have begun to think he had outlived his time.

His son and heir, Peada, had converted to Christianity as a condition of his marriage to a Northumbrian princess. After the wedding his bride arrived in Repton with four priests in tow. One of the quartet, Diuma, became the first Bishop of Mercia after Penda's death.

A monastery was established at Repton in AD 653 that prospered for two centuries until it was destroyed by an invading army of Danes. A priory was subsequently built in the 12th century and Repton's famous public school now occupies the site along with many other buildings scattered around the village. Through the 14th century gateway that is now a school entrance, next to St Wystan's church, there is a good view of buildings with early stone and brickwork.

At 212 feet, the lofty spire of St Wystan's makes a good match with that of St Oswald's church at Ashbourne. Unfortunately, in battle Oswald did not make quite such a good match for Penda, who personally saw he was despatched on his way to early canonisation. Concealed so completely beneath the north chapel of St Wystan's until it was inadvertently stumbled upon in the 18th century is a wonderful Saxon crypt. In this small space of elegant and restrained simplicity stone pillars carved with a spiral pattern support a vaulted roof. On each side, recesses are set into the 3 feet thick stone walls. This mausoleum of the royal house of Mercia incredibly survived the destruction of the monastery.

Dismiss the Anglo-Saxon age as crude and barbaric if you wish. But the crypt at Repton is witness to an alternative view of the so-called 'Dark Ages'. It is also worth noting that an abbess was in charge of the mixed monastic community founded here in the 7th century. Sexual equality was not an issue in Anglo-Saxon England. Yet as recently as 1848, a man led his wife to Repton cross and sold her to the highest bidder.

RIDDINGS

—— Coal mining and pig iron transformed Riddings from rural hamlet to industrial village two centuries ago. An investigation into some troublesome black ooze in the underground workings turned out to be the country's first oil strike and was refined as a lubricant and to produce paraffin for lamps. James Oakes, from Derby, took over the local ironworks in their infancy and laid out a 300-acre park that preserved some of the countryside from industrialisation. His descendants turned even more to agricultural pursuits and built Riddings Farm. This is now Park Mews, converted into private housing. From the path outside it is clear the farmyard layout remains substantially unchanged. An unusual octagonal granary occupies a central position in the cobbled yard. Nearby there is a water pump and a short curving stretch of narrow tramline that vanishes tantalisingly under a former barn door. The mews blend in with a delightfully tranquil old village centre hidden in a hollow, a world away from the undistinguished 20th century small town terraces and shop units that fill the surrounding outskirts.

A row of neat estate workers' cottages contemporary with the farm and an interesting assortment of older houses cluster around the former market place where a lane junction still frames a discernible triangular space. Of two public houses here, one is on the site of a former convent dedicated to St Mary Magdalene and claims to date from 1702. The other may possibly be Derbyshire's only thatched public house. Thatch is in fairly short supply throughout the county having largely given way to more durable slate as the roofing material of choice in the 16th century, a clue to the possible age of this building.

ROWARTH

—— As the patents on Arkwright's Water Frame and the innovations that followed on its heels expired, enterprising businessmen piled into cotton and the factory boom began in earnest. After a decade of planning, would-be cotton magnates had scouted for sites, laid plans and were ready to go. Isolated farming communities, where for centuries life had revolved around the land and the changing seasons, found industry appearing on their doorsteps almost overnight. Rowarth, two miles north of New Mills, was typical of the hamlets ripe for exploitation, a loose scatter of remote farms with the essential reliable flow of water in Rowarth Brook, tumbling down from Cown Edge Rocks.

The first waterwheel turned at Rowarth in 1781. Within a short time, four more mills were in operation. Cottages, public houses and a chapel to accommodate the influx of workers followed. But bubbles burst. Decline began as early as the 1820s and it came as swiftly and with all the drama and urgency that had accompanied Rowarth's expansion. Once steam superseded waterpower, Rowarth's natural resources were no longer sufficient to outweigh the disadvantages of inaccessibility.

Even today, Rowarth is delightfully isolated on a dead end road in the middle of nowhere with no railway and no canal. A seclusion that means it is not a village encountered by chance but, set in scenic hill country, it is well worth a visit. A walk around the village soon reveals the clues to Rowarth's enterprising past. Little Mill Inn at the southerly end of the village occupies the site of the first mill in the area. From here Chimney Path leads to what became the village centre in the boom years. There is no chimney to see now but the lines of a former reservoir can still be made out in a field to the right hand side of the path. Poplar Row, a run of nine cottages, contains some of the houses built in the early 19th century specifically to house the families coming into the area to work in the mills.

SAWLEY

—— Sawley, nowadays tacked seamlessly on to the south edge of neighbouring Long Eaton, with whom it once shared an important lace making industry, was once independent enough to have its own assize. All Saints' is a large, airy parish church built in a mixture of styles from Norman to Perpendicular and approached along a fine avenue of lime trees.

Today, Sawley is dominated by one of Europe's largest pleasure boat marinas. Moorings have expanded over the years taking over the pits left by gravel extraction. Sawley Marina continues a history of nautical activity in the area that stretches back at least to the Roman age and probably earlier. In prehistoric times transport by water was the quickest and safest way to travel. Lock Lane follows the route of an old Roman road to Trent Lock. Here, two public houses stand where the rivers Derwent and Soar together with the Erewash Canal meet in a spaghetti junction of waterways flowing into a broad beautiful curve of the Trent.

Large numbers of draught horses were kept to haul cargo upriver. The sight of unattended animals feeding from containers draped around their muzzles, while their handlers disappeared in search of their own refreshment, led to the 19th century inhabitants of Sawley being nicknamed 'nosebaggers'.

SHARDLOW

—— Until the head of navigation was extended for a brief period into Staffordshire, Shardlow, south-east of Derby, marked the limit for commercial traffic on the river Trent. For many years, trade on the river between here and Nottingham was a monopoly owned and fiercely guarded by the Fosbrook family. Leonard Fosbrook built Shardlow Hall from the profits in 1684. The hall is now a corporate headquarters and the view from the road is of the back of the hall because of a route diversion since the hall was first built.

When the Trent and Mersey Canal bypassed the lower reaches of the Trent to link back into the river at nearby Wilne, Shardlow's importance as an inland terminal port was reaffirmed. From its wharves a vast range of products including iron, cheese, beer, salt, pottery and timber were carried in single-masted ketches to the North Sea coastal ports. From there, the British merchant fleet transported them to markets around the world.

Shardlow Hall, former merchants' houses such as Broughton House and the Lady in Grey, and rows of workers' cottages reflect the growth and prosperity of Shardlow's 19th century heyday as a major inland port. Population growth outpaced facilities and before the village could afford its own parish church a boat was pressed into service each Sunday to ferry locals upstream to attend services at nearby Aston-on-Trent.

Most of the original wharves have disappeared but some red-brick warehouses, many of them featuring characteristic semicircular fanlight windows, still stand and there is a busy marina for modern pleasure craft. A former salt store, the Clock Warehouse, dating from 1780, has been converted into a heritage centre. This is built across an arm of the canal, an arrangement that allowed narrow boats to be unloaded directly into the store.

Just outside the village is Cavendish Bridge, named after the Duke of Devonshire, who built a tollbridge here in 1771. The Duke's bridge was washed away when the river flooded in 1947, and the modern structure is its replacement. An inscribed stone rescued from the now demolished tollhouse lists the cost of crossing the river in the days when a rope-hauled ferry or toll bridge were the only dry options for people and their animals. Foot passengers were charged a penny; cows crossed at a halfpenny each; coaches paid half a crown. This must have netted a fair return on the Duke's original outlay of £3,000 to build the bridge. Particularly so considering it was on the main coach route from Manchester to London, a journey that in 1771 had recently been significantly reduced thanks to road improvements, from three days to just two.

SMISBY

Tiny Smisby is just on the Derbyshire side of the county boundary with Leicestershire in pretty countryside that is largely unknown outside the local area. A church of grey sandstone stands on a low ridge at the end of the village where three roads meet. Beside the pavement nearby is a brick lock-up of the type commonly known as a 'roundhouse' even though

The roundhouse lock-up at Smisby.

they are often not circular. This example at Smisby is octagonal with a tall conical roof, no window and a still sturdy door of oak planks. Lock-ups of this type date from around 1770. They were in regular use for sixty years and occasionally called on afterwards by parish constables dispensing local justice by locking up those temporarily the worse for drink.

Petty criminals on their way to the Derby Assize courts could expect an overnight stay. So also could any unfortunate strangers discovered without the means to pay for food and lodging. From Elizabethan times until the reforms of the 19th century individual parishes were responsible for poor relief. They did not take kindly to sponsoring outsiders and a night in the lock-up faced the penniless traveller without the necessary papers confirming his home village would pick up any bill for upkeep. Vagrancy, as the 'crime' was described, was also punishable by flogging.

The area around Smisby provided the historical frame around which Sir Walter Scott draped the exciting fiction of *Ivanhoe*. Five minutes stroll south of the village, along Annwell Lane, there is an area of countryside with permitted public access. From here, the earthworks where a medieval manor once stood can be seen. Between this spot and the village is thought to be the site of the Tournament Field, mentioned by Scott, where knights from the nearby castle at Ashby-de-la-Zouch held their jousts.

SNELSTON

Snuggled enchantingly in a circle of hills on which fast flowing brooks rise, appearing and disappearing as they gather to flow into the nearby river Dove, Snelston, just off the A515 south of Ashbourne, is a designer village. Despite the impression created by intricate leaded windows and tall Tudor style chimneys, the cluster of red-brick houses at the village centre were nearly all built in the 1820s.

Beneath the overlay of a 19th century, planned country sporting estate with a wide variety of mature trees and numerous coverts are signs of an older Snelston. There are sunken roads and occasional fragments of earthworks. From the footpath that leads from Windmill Lane towards Snelston Park the unmistakable elongated reversed 'S' shaped ridge and furrow patterns, where a medieval ploughman once tilled, are clearly visible on the south-facing slope opposite. A little further along this same path there is the unexpected sight of a copse of monkey-puzzle trees. Rising to 100 feet high, the distinctive silhouette of their scaly-leaved branches lends a surreal touch of the exotic to the Derbyshire countryside. Introduced to England by Archibald Menzies, botanist and surgeon on the *Discovery* in 1795, the Chile pine (properly *Araucaria araucana* after the indigenous Araucanian people of South America) quickly gained popularity but is more usually grown as a single specimen.

The monkey-puzzle trees are not the only surprise. A little further on the footpath enters a covert by a unique wooden stile. Of three upright posts, one end is sawn into sections allowing the horizontal bars to travel along a groove cut in the opposite side via a pivot post. A light touch and all the bars seesaw down ready to be stepped over.

The unusual stile to be seen at Snelston.

SNITTERTON

—— The road here climbs the contours out of the Derwent Valley, well above the flood line that made travel on lower paths unpredictable before the Upper Derwent Valley dams calmed the river a century ago. This was the route followed by coach travellers on the Newhaven to Nottingham turnpike set up by an Act of Parliament in 1759.

Snitterton Hall is a beautiful Grade 1 listed building built in 1631, secluded from the road but visible from a footpath leading up onto Bonsall Moor. Signs of settlement long before the hall was built are all around. Constant ploughing until the Middle Ages has left its mark in the ridge and furrow patterns that corrugate the fields and on the lynchet (see Priestcliffe entry) terraces of the slopes. Beside the road next to Manor Farm look out for the site of the manor itself; long since disappeared but with the clear outline of its square moat and the depressions of fishponds that supplied the kitchen. We tend to associate moats with castles. In fact, such additions were a common feature of substantial 13th and 14th century properties. Those homesteads belonging to the strata of society we might today call the 'middle classes'. Why they became so popular is not clear. As a barrier a moat may have offered some protection against thieves or four-legged pests such as mice and rats. It may simply have been that they were fashionable. A medieval equivalent of 'keeping up with the Joneses'.

SOMERSAL HERBERT

—— Whichever route is chosen, the approach to secluded Somersal Herbert follows narrow, winding, hedge-squeezed lanes. This is a singularly quiet place with a sprinkle of half-timbered houses and a real gem at its centre in Somersal Herbert Hall. This brick and timber, gabled mansion dates from Tudor times. It incorporates both curved and straight beams within its box-framed pattern and is justifiably acclaimed as an example of Elizabethan style unmatched anywhere in the county. Built in 1564 by John Fitzherbert, probably to replace an earlier

Somersal Herbert Hall.

structure, the hall remained in the same family until a generation ago. It is still in private hands but a respectfully unobtrusive glimpse can be had through its gated entrance from the road leading to the nearby church.

SPONDON

—— Derbyshire can boast a fine collection of preaching crosses dating from the Anglo-Saxon age. Variously carved with interlace and knot work patterns, symbolic figures and religious scenes they show a high degree of craftsmanship. The preferred material was tough millstone grit, but occasionally sandstone was used as an alternative. You can see why in this suburb of Derby. In the churchyard at St Werburgh's, the Mercian kingdom's first home grown saint, the decoration on the remains of a cross-shaft made, uncommonly, of limestone has been so weathered it is now illegible.

STANTON-IN-THE-PEAK

—— It was once common practice for commercial buildings to display signs for those unable to read and inn signs have a long history. The oldest public house names can be traced back to the days of the Roman Empire and ancient Egypt. In later times it became common to use references to a wide range of subjects. For example, sport, royalty, famous people and events, or location — but The Flying Childers? The answer is that it is a tribute to a famous racehorse bought as a 5-year-old in 1719 by William Cavendish, 2nd Duke of Devonshire. The Flying Childers swept all before it at Newmarket where it was reputed to be 'The fleetest horse that ever ran'. A portrait of the horse hangs in the west entrance hall at Chatsworth House.

STANTON MOOR

—— Is it just imagination that gives this heather-cloaked gritstone plateau such a strong atmospheric undertow? What is inescapable is its importance to our ancestors. Amongst the collection of prehistoric remains on its 150 acres near Birchover, are at least 70 burial cairns, Nine Ladies stone circle and King's Stone. Following extensive excavation (the finds can be seen in Sheffield Museum) each cairn now displays an individual number. Nature clearly provided inspiration for human endeavour here. Occasional gritstone blocks rise from the ground in incredible and strange shapes. They have been given names like 'Cork Stone', 'Andle Stone' and 'Cat Stone' and are major features on the landscape.

Quarrying has gnawed away at the south-western corner of the moor, an activity that has left an interesting legacy largely ignored by those who visit this popular spot. In disused workings behind a wire fence close to the Cork Stone are a small pile of part-completed millstones stacked like some giant coinage on the quarry floor. It is almost as if the workmen have only temporarily downed tools and may return at any moment to finish the job. Clearly the quarrymen worked until the last minute hoping for a revival in dwindling demand that never materialised. We can imagine their last few days' wages proved equally elusive.

Cutting millstones was a highly skilled job. The gritstone slab sections had to be carefully chosen from fault-free sections and carefully cut from the rock face. Each stone was accurately chiselled into a circular shape before final precision dressing. Millstones work in pairs. The bottom stone has furrows cut in a pattern of intersecting triangular shaped segments known as 'harps'. One side of the furrow is vertical; the other chamfered to produce a scissor action as the top stone turns. The grooves allow the grain to be milled without the flour clogging the stones. They grind ever finer as the meal is channelled to the outer skirt of the stones where it is discharged for bagging.

This abandoned quarry is a reminder of what was once a major business based on one of Derbyshire's richest natural resources.

STEETLEY

—— Why a tiny gem of a church with peerless decorative stonework representing the pinnacle of Norman architectural achievement should be tucked away in this obscure corner of Derbyshire is a question that has puzzled people for many years. Steetley chapel, built around 1120, is barely 18 paces long and lucky to survive. Until 10 years of careful restoration was completed in 1880 it was a roofless ruin doubling as a cowshed. According to folklore, Robin Hood and his band worshipped here, but it is the extravagant ornamentation and intricate architectural detail that attracts people.

Also worthy of attention but missed by most visitors is a dovecote that remains amongst the converted buildings of nearby Steetley Farm. It was the Normans who made dovecotes popular, building functional, sturdy structures with a honeycomb of nest holes on the inner walls. Pigeons were an important source of fresh meat in the days before winter fodder, when apart from essential breeding stock, animals were slaughtered each autumn. Basic design changed little over the years making dating difficult but this particular dovecote is undoubtedly ancient and was probably built at the same time as the chapel.

STONEY MIDDLETON

— Quarrying and the disused shafts of former lead mines, many with spoil heaps subsequently reworked for fluorspar, hem around 'Stoney' on the busy A623. Fluorspar was treated as waste by the lead miners. Later it was discovered to be an efficient flux useful in steel making and yesterday's rubbish became valuable. This mining backdrop makes the Nook, a leafy tranquil square on the north-east fringe of the village, even more unexpected. Here you will find the only octagonal church in the county, tacked on to a square tower that pre-dates the church itself. Inside the pews are arranged to face inwards offering a kind of 'sermon in the round' experience for the congregation. Each July, the two wells close to the church are blessed and decorated with flowers following Derbyshire's unique well dressing customs.

Next to a hall in the Nook is a renovated spring-fed bath house. Known as the Roman Bath, its thermal qualities may have attracted use from early times. There is said to have been a Roman settlement here but a convincing site has yet to be identified. The restoration we can see today is most likely a relic of the late 18th century fashion for 'taking the waters', exploited most successfully in Derbyshire at Buxton and Matlock.

Around the turn of the 18th century Stoney was an important centre and one of no more than a dozen places in the county enjoying a daily postal service from London. By the time the Turnpike Trust met, in the Moon Inn, to agree the building of a tollhouse in the village, having eight sides had obviously caught the local imagination. An octagonal, single-storey tollhouse was built in 1840, over the brook in the village centre where it still stands. For a tollhouse, the shape had some practical advantages. The keeper could see travellers coming from every direction. Mail coaches, however, for whom speed was of the essence were legally exempt from toll fees and would announce their approach with a sharp blast on the post horn in order that the gate could be opened in readiness.

❧ SUDBURY

It took George Vernon thirty years to complete Sudbury Hall. His grandmother had begun the original building early in the 17th century but it was George who masterminded the realisation of this treasure of a house in the form we see today — pretty much rebuilding the village as well while he was about it. Craftsmen of the highest quality were employed on the project, including the most famous woodcarver of his day, Grinling Gibbons, and it shows. Masters of their trade created a sumptuous interior of lavish decorative woodwork and elaborate plaster. Some had honed their skills working at Chatsworth House, others with Sir Christopher Wren. Since 1967, the National Trust has owned and looked after the property.

The bricks for Sudbury Hall were produced on the spot in temporary kilns from local clay. A higher firing temperature produced the darker, 'blued' bricks used in the distinctive external diamond pattern. Around the corner, in School Lane, the diaper brickwork is copied in a more modest building that was originally the gas works supplying the hall.

High walls or tall gates guard many great houses from public view. There are no such trappings at Sudbury and the hall stands in open view from the village street. With the house so dominant it is no surprise that other attractive features can go unremarked. Stand with your back to the hall and look half a mile away across the busy A50 to see what appears to be a low, battlemented brick 'fortress' with a square tower planted at each corner. This is a deercote, built when every self-respecting landowner kept a herd of fallow deer.

The rooftops of Sudbury receive little attention but are also interesting. Flanking the cupola above the hall notice the elegant broad chimneys of a design known as 'Tea Caddy' stacks, the name deriving from their shape. On the roof of the Vernon Arms, a former coaching stop opposite the hall, the chimneys are a fine example of midland star pattern, a definitive East Midlands regional style rare outside the area.

SUTTON-ON-THE-HILL

—— The spire of St Michaels' church on a slight ridge in the flat agricultural landscape of fields and hedgerows can be seen for some distance. If you are lucky enough to find it open look for the memorials to the Sleigh family and in particular Sir Samuel's alabaster testimonial.

Sir Samuel Sleigh was a lawyer and among the first men in Derbyshire to stand up and be counted for the Parliamentarian cause in the Civil War. Being on the winning side enabled him to force the sale of Etwall Hall from its Royalist occupant. He then set about extending his new home using Tutbury Castle, just across the county line in Staffordshire, as a convenient source of ready dressed stone. He justified his action on the grounds that he was ensuring the King's soldiers could make no further use of the castle as a stronghold. In 1648 he became County Sheriff of Derby.

As the days of the Commonwealth came to an end, Sir Samuel successfully anticipated the mood of the times, declared his support for the Restoration and was duly reappointed to his post as County Sheriff by the new monarch, Charles II.

Clearly our man was not only able but also had considerable personal charm, which brings me to the point. The memorials show Sir Samuel had three wives. He died in 1679 and never saw Mary, the daughter who eventually succeeded to his estates. Check the dates. Incredibly, more than a century separates the death of the first Lady Sleigh and the last.

SUTTON SCARSDALE

—— Keep your eyes on the road but the romantic ruins of Sutton Scarsdale Hall may be glimpsed from the M1 motorway close to junction 29. Distance lends an impression of romantic splendour. In reality the great house is now a robbed out hollow shell of the once grand mansion redesigned by Nicholas Leake, 4th and last Earl of Scarsdale, in 1724. No expense was spared in the building. The Earl was a man of his age, captivated by the extravagant fashions, moods and manners of the time.

Whatever the truth about his lifestyle he enjoyed himself sufficiently to die bankrupt, and allegedly provided engraver and painter William Hogarth with the model for his dissolute, high-living peer satirically depicted in *The Rake's Progress*. It is this fictional coding of Sutton Scarsdale Hall and of the surrounding area that is the hidden feature here. Not just in the work of Hogarth, but most especially in D. H. Lawrence's *Lady Chatterley's Lover*.

From 1824 until 1920, the Arkwright family lived at Sutton Scarsdale. The hall is thinly disguised as Fritchley in Lawrence's controversial novel, and the Arkwrights were transformed into the Weatherley family, though one member is said to have supplied the inspiration for the character of Sir Clifford Chatterley. After the Arkwrights left, a wealthy American buyer stripped Sutton Scarsdale Hall of its treasures and shipped them to a museum in Philadelphia. In the book, set in the years immediately after the First World War, Lady Constance bemoans the loss of 'England, my England!' as 'Fritchley, a perfect old Georgian Mansion, was even now, as Connie passed in the car, being demolished. It was in perfect repair: till the war the Weatherleys had lived in style there.'

Deciphering the real Derbyshire locations Lawrence featured in fictional form in the book can be an interesting diversion. Some are in thin disguise: Warsop Castle is Bolsover Castle; Chadwick Hall is Hardwick Hall; and Uthwaite, with its '... pathetic little corkscrew spire of the church, that is going to tumble down ...' is clearly Chesterfield. Others may take a little more detective work to uncover.

SWADLINCOTE

—— Coal and clay took their toll on the landscape of much of south-west Derbyshire. Heavy, primary industries largely defined the culture of the area until recent times. Now Swadlincote is in 'recovery' and its character is in transition. At the heart of the new National Forest, a multitude of saplings have been planted in great swathes across set-aside rural and brownfield sites alike.

At the same time, not all the signs of Swadlincote's rich working heritage are being swept away. On the edge of the town centre, the characteristic bottle-shaped silhouette of a kiln hovel for firing pottery stands as a reminder. Pottery was stacked inside the kiln and the door sealed with clay before firing. The outer hovel protected the kiln and helped contain the fierce temperatures generated. The bottle shape encouraged an efficient updraught, in the space between the kiln and the hovel walls.

Sharpe's Pottery Works remarkably survived virtually unaltered from the 1820s, the days immediately after the dandifications of Regency fashion, until they closed down commercially at the height of a similarly fashion-conscious decade, the 'swinging' 1960s. The works are now the focal point of a local conservation area in the process of being restored and converted into a resource centre that will celebrate the area's proud industrial past.

In the course of its working life, the bottle kiln adapted to changes in demand and emerging markets. A wide variety of goods were produced from tableware to, perhaps most significantly, water closets. Community health became an increasing issue as the population expanded in Victorian times. Sanitation was a concern not just of the poor forced to live in crowded conditions but for all. Action for improvements was given an added impetus by the premature death of Prince Albert, allegedly connected to Windsor Castle's antiquated sewage system, followed a few years later by the Prince of Wales contracting typhoid fever. Water closets had been around at the top end of the housing market since the 1770s but with unventilated pipes connecting to cess-pits they were probably more of a danger than the backyard privies enjoyed, and frequently shared, by the majority of the population. It was a century later before the modern washdown system was introduced. The Public Health Act (1875) led to the development of municipal water supplies and sewers and ensured the widespread popularity of flush toilets linked to a sewage disposal system.

Sharpe's of Swadlincote were market leaders in WC design, producing the finest bowls with delicate flower designs fit to grace any 'convenience' or 'thunderbox'.

SWARKESTONE

There has been a stone bridge spanning the river Trent at Swarkestone for at least eight centuries. A wooden structure probably existed earlier. River crossings always have a story to tell. This one includes a tragic romantic legend, civil war, and the end of a doomed revolutionary adventure.

The present bridge was built in 1801, reusing some of the stone from its medieval predecessor. It was on the main route from Derby to London and mail coaches crossed regularly. Nearby, the Georgian Crewe and Harpur Inn prospered from the passing trade. Over the bridge, Swarkestone is linked to its neighbour, Stanton by Bridge, along a narrow causeway that stretches ribbon-like for three-quarters of a mile across the flood plain. According to legend, two sisters of noble family had the bridge built after their impatient lovers drowned attempting to visit the girls at their Swarkestone home when the river Trent was in full spate. The story adds that the expense ruined the family and reduced the girls to poverty for the rest of their lives.

During the Civil War, Sir John Harpur fortified the bridge to prevent the Parliamentarians crossing. Unfortunately, he found himself up against the redoubtable Derbyshire Roundhead Sir John Gell, a man of considerable military skill who was not above using the conflict to pursue a personal animosity against the county's gentry. Gell routed the Royalist forces and took the opportunity to demolish Swarkestone Hall, the Harpur family home. All that remains of the hall is an unimpressive stretch of wall and fragments of outbuilding. But Gell left standing an improbably ornate Jacobean pavilion sited incongruously in the centre of what became known as Balcony Field overlooking the 'Cuttle', a walled enclosure about the size of a football pitch. The building, sympathetically restored by the Landmark Trust, consists of two linked turrets of three storeys. The turrets are reminiscent of the Hunting Tower in Chatsworth Park, one of the few surviving buildings from Bess of Hardwick's first Chatsworth House. Speculation about its purpose includes suggestions that it was a hunting lodge offering views of the chase or that it was a grandstand for spectators of whatever activity took place in the Cuttle. The odds are that an early form of bowls called Pell Mell, popular in the 17th century, was played in the Cuttle field. This theory is supported by a surviving record of a payment made in 1632 in respect of a 'bowle alley house'. Deer coursing, a very popular spectator sport of the time, is a less savoury possibility. For this diversion, greyhounds were used to pursue and kill deer. Deer are pacy sprinters but their stamina fades after a mile or so enabling a course to be calculated over which the deer are chased towards the spectators and the bloody finale enacted in gory close-up.

The strategic importance of Swarkestone Bridge was emphasised when Bonnie Prince Charlie arrived in Derby with his Highland army in December 1745. An advance force was sent to secure the crossing and Charles Edward Stuart might have come here himself to gaze along the causeway and ponder his future. Had he crossed history might have been rewritten.

The Jacobean pavilion at Swarkestone.

There was plenty of evidence pointing to panic in London and King George II had laid plans for escape. As it was, the Jacobites turned back at Swarkestone, to make their last stand four months later at Culloden.

It may be a registered ancient monument freighted with the weight of a colourful history, but Swarkestone causeway still does its day job, carrying a regular flow of modern traffic over its venerable stones.

TADDINGTON

Springs and wells have been venerated from the earliest of times. Celtic spirits were believed to inhabit water, as well as trees and other natural objects. It is a legacy that lives on in Derbyshire's famous well dressing ceremonies. Drinking water for people and for livestock was an important commodity in the limestone uplands where any rainfall drains quickly through the porous bedrock. Ten minutes uphill walk from the village centre is Taddington's High Well. Recently restored after years of neglect following connection of the village to a mains water supply, it is now dressed annually each August, but receives few visitors at other times and is easily missed.

Positioned in the centre of high limestone country, Taddington is a good centre from which to search out examples of another watery White Peak speciality. In the surrounding upland fields, most usually in the lowest corner, meres can be found — small, circular ponds built to catch rainwater. Until the arrival of piped water in the 1930s mere making was an important local craft. Originally, meres were made watertight by puddling clay and straw underfoot — a little like treading grapes. Concrete, once available, soon took over. Mere builders worked in pairs, travelling the area to dig and maintain these vital, but largely unnoticed, farm features.

The A6 runs between the wooded slopes of Taddington Dale down into the Wye Valley and on to Bakewell. A car park at the foot of the incline gives access northwards to Monsal Dale. But there is much of interest in the opposite direction. Follow the edge of Taddington Wood into the steep gorge of Deep Dale with caves, a rock shelter and the humps and bumps of a long abandoned settlement at its head.

THORPE

Thorpe is an unassuming but pretty little village largely ignored by the crowds who flock through en route to the rather more spectacular delights of Dovedale. The sheer number of visitors to the dale is a problem for the Peak Park authorities. The footpath to the summit of Thorpe Cloud, the village's dominating backdrop, has become so badly eroded that sections have had to be fenced off and re-routed. It is well worth leaving the crowds behind and exploring the area away from such well-trodden paths.

St Leonard's church was rebuilt in the 19th century but retains a Norman tower and recessed, two-light windows in the belfry that are typical of earlier, Saxon designs. Look out for a vertical sundial in the churchyard, made by Derby watchmaker John Whitehurst in the 18th century and set so high it is easily missed and may have been intended to be read from horseback or from the driving seat of a coach.

The busy turnpike road from Ashbourne once ran close by the church. The old route now forms part of the Limestone Way footpath. A 10-minute stroll south-west along this track brings you to deserted Coldwall Bridge. It is dated 1762 but this is probably when the structure was renovated. A milestone from 1822 records: Cheadle, 11 miles. The bridge is well buttressed with a single arch spanning the river Dove. Motor vehicles last crossed here in Edwardian times. The engines in those early models must have struggled to cope with the steep incline out of the river valley. Today it is as quiet and pleasant a spot as could be desired.

ꙮ Ticknall

⎯ With the entrance to Calke Abbey leading off its main street, many visitors drive straight through this delightful village situated 8 miles south of Derby. Ticknall once had a thriving brickyard making use of local clay deposits and its older timber-framed cottages reflect the local product. Century old cast iron water pumps, a gift from the Harpur Crewe family of Calke Abbey, dot the streets.

Near St George's church stand a group of almshouses, built in 1772 for — as it was described at the time — 'seven decayed housekeepers', formerly servants at Calke Abbey. The church, built 70 years after the almshouses, has fragments of a tower belonging to a 14th century predecessor still standing in its grounds. This earlier model was so solidly built that demolition necessitated recourse to explosives.

Set back so unobtrusively into a wall on Main Street and partly obscured by foliage is a stone roundhouse with a typically conical roof and studded oak door. It was formerly used as an overnight lock-up for drunks and vagrants (see Smisby entry).

Close to the Calke Abbey drive, the arch of Horseshoe Bridge that once carried a tramway spans the main road. Until 1913, horses regularly hauled trucks, freighted with coal inwards and bricks and clay outwards, along its rails. Spurs from the tramline gave access to the canal system in nearby Leicestershire.

Although a quiet rural backwater today, Ticknall was once a busy working village. As well as brickmaking the local clay supported pottery manufacture and limestone was quarried in industrial quantities. Traces of the former lime workings can still be seen, overgrown and flooded now, beside a footpath that leads to Staunton Harold Reservoir. The last limekiln firing in Ticknall took place in 1940. By then the industry was all but finished and World War II signalled the end. The glow from a burning kiln would have acted like a beacon at night for enemy aircraft, posing an unacceptable risk as the German Luftwaffe increased the intensity of bombing raids.

Ruined fragments of St George's 14th century predecessor in the churchyard at Ticknall.

TIDESWELL

This large, grey stone village at the centre of the Peak District National Park hemmed in by the high limestone ridges of Longstone Edge and Hucklow Edge promotes itself as 'Derbyshire's best kept secret'. Many early trackways and Peak District routes met here and made this an important centre in medieval times. In the 13th century Tideswell was the main administrative centre for the Royal Forest of the Peak. If the village's main charm is that it has retained a typical Peakland feel, untouched by fads and fashions, its greatest asset is undoubtedly the glorious church of St John the Baptist. Known deservedly as 'the Cathedral of the Peak', it is a masterpiece of symmetry, 145 feet in length with an imposing square tower rising to a height of 100 feet.

St John's has remained largely unchanged since the 14th century. Inside it is a treasure house of pre-Reformation monuments, old and new stained glass windows and some unmissable 19th century wood carving, much of it by local craftsman Advent Hunstone, including most notably the vicar's chair below the pulpit and the organ surround.

Amongst several monuments in the church look out for the tomb of Sir Sampson Meverill in the centre of the chancel. Sir Sampson was born in Tideswell about the same time as the church was completed. He became a famous soldier campaigning with Henry V in France and probably fighting at Agincourt. The engraving on the brass plate shows a representation of the Holy Trinity very similar in design to that on the tomb of Edward the Black Prince in Canterbury Cathedral.

What remains completely hidden in the churchyard, buried in an unmarked grave, is the head of Catholic martyr Nicholas Garlick whose fate is recounted in the entries for Derby and Padley.

TINTWISTLE

Tintwistle is on the north-western boundary of the Peak Park in the Etherow Valley. 'Top End', the oldest part of this tiny gritstone village has stocks and a well. Rows of weavers' cottages here are a reminder of the 18th century cotton boom when outworkers were employed to knit yarn on hired stocking frames while their families worked in the spinning mills. According to local legend, Dick Turpin, the infamous highwayman, had his horse shod backwards at Tintwistle to confuse pursuers.

This is a good place to explore Longdendale and some of the most wild, open countryside in Derbyshire — so secluded that a fortified site overlaid by more recent field enclosures near Highstones, above Torside Reservoir, went unnoticed until a few years ago. The site, next to a footpath and less than 200 yards from the Pennine Way, was dismissed as a spread of debris left by a retreating glacier after the last ice age. It is now thought to be of possible Roman or Iron Age origin. Backed by inhospitable moorland heath it is halfway up an incline rather than on a highpoint but has a commanding position. From behind the 30 feet wide earthwork rampart and encircling V-shaped ditch, movements both up and down the valley, which was an important trade route from east to west, and north along Crowden Brook could be monitored.

TISSINGTON

Turning off from the A515 Ashbourne to Buxton road the approach to Tissington leads between imposing stone gateposts and then along a lime-fringed avenue. It feels a little as if trespassing in a private world. From this direction, Tissington Hall grounds can be seen to the left. A footpath that skirts the estate boundary here follows the line of a ha-ha, or hidden ditch, designed to keep out livestock without spoiling the view. The idea for these once fashionable landscape features came from France early in the 18th century. Entering Tissington, a row of red-brick former railway houses at the edge of the village look a little out of place. But the village itself is a Derbyshire dream wrapped around 17th century Tissington Hall and complete with duck pond. Low stone walls and broad green verges add to a sense of airy openness. Often quiet, the famous Ascension Day well dressings turn it into a honey pot for visitors.

St Mary's church, extensively restored but with some traces of its Norman origins remaining, stands on a rise of land slightly apart from the village. This area used to be the focal point of the community. Before the current hall was built a medieval manor house stood immediately north of the church. Rarely noticed shadowy earthworks are still visible showing the site of this early manor.

Do not miss the curious indentations in the stonework around the south doorway arch of St Mary's. These are the marks left by the sharpening of arrowheads. Shooting off arrows in the churchyard may seem like an impious act but in the past a close connection existed between the church and skill with the longbow. In the 14th century, all able-bodied men were expected to ensure they were proficient with the longbow, ready to be called up in the case of a national emergency. By royal decree, Sunday afternoon was set aside for archery practice. Spare bows and arrows for those without weapons of their own were stored in churches and targets were commonly set up in the churchyard.

TWO DALES

Now an integral part of Darley Dale, Two Dales, known less romantically as 'Toadholes' until quite late in the 19th century, is a quiet spot wrapped around a loop of road leading off from the B5057 to Chesterfield. It is not much visited except by those who live there. The basement of Georgian Holt House was once a bank. A pleasant short walk leads along the steep valley of tiny Sydnope Brook with an attractive waterfall and where Potter Dam and Fancy Dam create small lakes. Three dams on the brook once combined to raise a head of water close to 100 feet in order to power a flax spinning operation. Coping with such water pressure required the mill owners to design a special engine for the job. The gritstone mill of Edward and James Dukayne still stands but its commercial operations have changed to dealing in animal feed.

UNTHANK

—— Do not blink and miss Unthank if you happen to be travelling along the road that marks the eastern boundary of the Peak District National Park between Barlow and Ramsley Moor. The name derives from old English and translates as 'not granted' or 'unacknowledged', suggesting that whoever successfully first acquired the land on which the hall now stands was an enterprising squatter rather than a legitimate inheritor or purchaser.

Old houses develop over time. Most contain a mix of architectural styles reflecting different periods and yet somehow still manage to add up to a uniform whole. Unthank Hall is typical of properties with generations of occupation. It almost certainly has parts that date back to the 15th century integrated with later additions. A two-storey outbuilding may be even earlier. A large barn is divided into bays by five sets of cruck frames (see Osmaston entry). Not so long ago, before the days of farm mechanisation, this barn would have echoed each autumn to the rhythmic thump of flails as corn was threshed, with doors flung wide to catch the breeze that aided the winnowing of chaff from grain in a time-honoured way unchanged for centuries.

UPPER DERWENT VALLEY

—— An army of navvies began building the first dam here for the local water company a century or so ago. The heartbeat current of the river Derwent now pulses watery life into Howden, Derwent and Ladybower reservoirs in turn. When Ladybower was filled, in 1945, the villages of Ashopton and Derwent Woodlands vanished Atlantis-like in the flood. But not quite all traces disappeared. A character known as 'Peeping Tom', a statue peering over a wall that once amused and surprised callers at

Derwent Hall, was rescued and can now be seen in his new home at the National Park Information Centre. A war memorial was transferred to safety higher up the valley slope. Most satisfyingly, a two-arched, 17th century packhorse bridge was carefully dismantled, stone by stone, and rebuilt jigsaw fashion on the same packhorse route further north. This now spans the river Derwent at Slippery Stones, half a mile beyond the limit of Howden Reservoir, and can be reached by a track that takes over from the road following the river's eastern flank.

Above these Upper Derwent lakes the pilots of the Royal Air Force's 'Dambusting' Lancaster Bomber team honed their low level flying skills before setting off to skim Barnes Wallis's bouncing bombs to such devastatingly destructive effect along the Ruhr Valley. With twin tower turrets, Derwent Dam presented a good approximation of the German target. The movie of this intrepid wartime episode was also filmed here. Sir Barnes Wallis, incidentally, was born at Butterley, in Derbyshire.

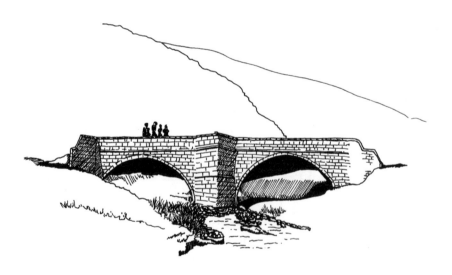

The 17th century packhorse bridge at Slippery Stones in the Upper Derwent Valley.

✿ UPPER LANGWITH

——— How much of our past still remains to be discovered? During the last ice age, more than 10,000 years ago, Derbyshire was just about the most northerly habitable place in Europe. Natural caves in the limestone ravine at Cresswell Crags, half in Derbyshire and half in Nottinghamshire, have yielded a wealth of finds including flint tools and carved bone ornaments. It would be hard to over-estimate the archaeological importance of this site. It is up there with Arbor Low and Stonehenge. Although the caves are now sealed a visitors' centre runs tours and mounts displays. Cresswell cannot be the only such site and other caves must await detection.

Not far away from Cresswell, much less well known and far less visited, is a cave close to Upper Langwith. Flint scrapers and a human skull were found inside when it was first discovered and explored, in 1903. The site is on the north bank of the river Poulter and close to the main A632 road but is best approached from Upper Langwith village. Follow a footpath beside the church and over the brow of a low hill. It is a short, pleasant stroll and unlike in the days of the cave's first prehistoric human occupants there is no risk of a chance encounter with a mammoth, sabre-tooth tiger or hyena.

✿ WALTON-ON-TRENT

——— Picture the scene: it is 1322 and the powerful Earl of Lancaster has barricaded a long narrow bridge across the river Trent. He and his forces are on the Staffordshire side thumbing their noses at King Edward II and his army on the Derbyshire bank, feeling relaxed and safe in the knowledge that the next nearest bridge is half a day's march away. More than a century has passed since the barons of England slipped a quill pen into King John's reluctant fist at Runnymede and pointed meaningfully to a dotted line at the foot of Magna Carta. Times have changed. The King's authority is more constrained. A parliament of knights and burgesses represent the shires but power struggles continue. Unable to penetrate the Earl's defensive wall, Edward is frustrated and desperate. Then his prayers are answered. Along comes someone with a little local knowledge of 'hidden Derbyshire' to whisper in the King's ear about a ford, just a stone's throw away, at this little place called Walton. Leaving enough men to keep the Earl's forces occupied, Edward and the remainder of his troops cross at Walton and put the rebels to flight. Another ambitious baron's revolt successfully overcome.

For light traffic there is now a Bailey bridge over the spot where the royal forces crossed the river. Large vehicles still face a significant detour at this tiny village with its own footnote to a turning point in history.

WARDLOW

———— There is nothing dramatic to attract the attention of a modern traveller at Wardlow. Its most significant landmark is a domed outcrop of limestone, Peter's Stone, on a ridge at the head of a path leading into the attractively wooded valley of Cressbrook Dale. The area does have another claim if not to fame, then at least to a passing mention in the annals of Derbyshire crime. In a field north of the T-junction at Wardlow Mires stood the last gibbet in the county.

A gibbet — the same etymological root gives us the word 'jib' used today to describe the arm of a crane — was a gallows for displaying the bodies of criminals after execution. Although intended as a grim warning to discourage anyone tempted to stray on the wrong side of the law, it does not seem to have been a very effective deterrent in these often desperate times. The packhorse trains that were a regular feature in the district into the mid 18th century were a prime target for highwaymen. The best known in this area, Black Harry, operated in the early 18th century at the same time as Dick Turpin was active elsewhere. An old packhorse route is still known for part of its length over Middleton Moor as 'Black Harry Lane'. Our man knew the terrain well and must have gazed at the gibbet many times, probably drinking at the tavern in its shadow. Eventually the law caught up with him and he met his own date with destiny, paying the price of his misdeeds at Wardlow Mires. The last person gibbeted here was Anthony Lingard, a young man from Tideswell, who murdered and robbed the Wardlow tollhouse keeper in 1815.

WENSLEY

——— Wensley is at the hub of some delightful countryside including its own Wensley Dale. A rural feature of the landscape it shares with its namesake in county neighbour Yorkshire is the occasional field barn that can be seen on the surrounding moorland.

Field barns were used as hay stores — many are equipped with wide double doors to allow access for hay carts — and to overwinter cattle. The poor soil of the high moors in this part of the county does not make for easy farming. By having a barn sited out in the fields farmers ensured hay could be quickly harvested and stored, thus minimising the time it lay out in unpredictable weather conditions and cutting down on transport. It meant hay was on hand for winter feed and the manure, produced by cattle housed in the barn for the winter, was also on site ready to be spread as fertiliser.

A secondary reason was that many farmers did not have farmhouses but lived in cottages in villages such as Wensley and walked to work on their land daily.

WESSINGTON

——— Wessington and its next door neighbour Brackenfield have both retained extensive village greens, bigger than any others remaining in the county. As common land it came in handy during the 19th century when coal seams beneath the green kept the village fires burning in times of hardship. The village's water supply also came from Tea, Moses and Jubilee, the three wells on the green.

Half a mile west of the village is Lindway Springs, a tiny patch of woodland where traces of Neolithic hut foundations were said to have been uncovered in the 1890s. Roundhouses from this period have been excavated elsewhere in the country and show they were built by wattling hazel branches around a circle of stakes to create walls that could be covered with a daub of mud and straw. Steep roofs were thatched with a broad overhang. The chief clues left behind from those early habitations that modern archaeologists use to reconstruct the past are the postholes where the stakes were hammered into the ground and hearthstones. Is this what was discovered here over a century ago? Or were the diggers fooled by traces of rather more modern activity — perhaps misinterpreting bellpits, similar to those a few miles away at Brimington, as echoes of antiquity?

WESTON-ON-TRENT

—— What was it that once attracted hundreds of visitors to Weston? It is small and neat with a mix of old and new properties, but these days more commuter village than rural community. Hard to believe it once buzzed with day-trippers. Stroll down King's Mill Lane and follow a path through the open meadows to a broad shining stretch of the river Trent. Here a grassy ridge on the opposite bank forms a verdant backdrop and the waters cascade in a curling rush over a weir. Tastes and times change but in the early years of the 20th century when people had little enough money to spare simple pleasures were embraced. World war, economic depression and high unemployment took their toll and this delightful spot offered people in the industrial towns — the centre of Derby is only 10 miles away — an escape from the factory chimneys and everyday cares.

King's Mill is the site of a ford. The river has shallows as well as deep water in which people paddled and swam. Upstream of the weir was a lido. Visitors could hire rowing boats or take a pleasure cruise further upriver to Black Pool, a tiny natural oxbow. On the banks people camped, sunbathed, picnicked and fished. Look out for traces of eel traps and of a chute that acted as a salmon leap. If recent reintroduction programmes are successful salmon may make a welcome return to the river after an absence of almost a century.

Regular overhead traffic from East Midlands Airport, barely 5 miles away as the jet flies, is a reminder of the range of exotic locations on offer today. There may be no pleasure boats now and swimming is definitely off the agenda but this is still an attractive spot to seek out.

Back in the village, behind the triangular green, the former Weston Hall is now an inn and restaurant. Fishing ponds have replaced the original encircling ditch but when the site was laid out the largest moat in Derbyshire was planned. The hall too would have been large and impressive but for the fact that its construction was interrupted by the Civil War and never completed. Instead, a new extension has been grafted onto what remains of the initial building.

WHATSTANDWELL

How did it get its name, this handful of houses and a bridge? The river crossing is the key. The first bridge here was built in the 14th century when the land belonged to the Augustinian monks of Darley Abbey. It is the spot where, because of the valley contours, the Matlock to Derby road crossed over from west of the river Derwent to hug the eastern bank. The bridge came to be known by the name of Walter Stonewell who happened to live nearby and by a process of Chinese whispers soon became Whatstandwell.

By the bridge are a hotel and a row of cottages with a well in the yard outside. Beside the hotel, do not miss the mounting block, a set of stone steps to help travellers in the days of horse transport to climb into the saddle. Mounting blocks were commonly found in public places, often next to churches or in market squares, from the Middle Ages until the 19th century. Now they are increasingly rare. There is another reminder of the days of real horsepower amongst the row of cottages. One of these was once a blacksmith's shop. Large, double access doors where the forge was housed can still be seen although the space has now been converted into a window.

WHITTINGTON

—— Old Whittington 1688: around a candlelit table in the cramped back room of the Cock and Pynot alehouse their lordships the Earl of Devonshire, the Earl of Danby and Lord Delamere are meeting in secret session. The topic? High treason, or so it would have been if the 'Glorious Revolution' had failed and William and Mary had not replaced James II on the throne of England. As it transpired the overthrow succeeded and the Earl of Devonshire was rewarded by a dukedom for his part in the coup. The Cock and Pynot is now Revolution House, a museum of the events but a surrogate tavern — updated as the Cock and Magpie — stands next to the site. And so this village played its part in the nation's history before retiring into obscurity as a suburb of Chesterfield.

Well, not quite obscurity. Whittington glassware became very popular in the 18th century. The works were able to take advantage of the Chesterfield Canal, surveyed by the pioneering James Brindley and opened in 1777 to coincide with the Trent and Mersey cross-country navigation links. This allowed the transport of fragile products safely to market. The canal is no longer used and the glassworks are gone but the footpath across Glasshouse Common follows the route of the horse-drawn tramway that led from the works to Dixon's Lock, near Hounsfield Bridge, where goods were loaded. Whittington glass products can still be seen in Chesterfield's museum.

WILLINGTON

—— Unless they are spectacular we tend to take road bridges for granted — a barely noticed means of getting from point A to point B. This is perhaps especially so when A and B are within shouting distance. Village neighbours Willington and Repton are scarcely a mile apart but before Willington Bridge was built the choice was a ferry or, for large loads, a detour by road that added over 20 miles to a round trip. Modern housing has encroached on Ferry Green but a footpath still leads to the place where the ferry operated. From this spot on the bank the needle thin spire of St Wystan's church at Repton piercing the skyline must have seen temptingly near to early travellers but the river here is wide.

Willington finally got its bridge in 1839, a graceful five-arched stone structure designed by James Trubshaw. Both villages celebrated the grand opening of the bridge but the festivities were nothing compared to the jubilation nearly 60 years later when money raised by local subscriptions freed the bridge from tolls. Small wonder that many tollhouses, symbols of an unpopular levy, fail to survive. All that now stands on the open platform where the fees charged for crossing Willington Bridge were collected is a commemorative board telling the story of the bridge.

WINSTER

A boom in lead mining during the 18th century brought the prosperity that is reflected in the refined quality of individual properties, intersected by cramped alleys rising steeply up the hillside. Most of the handsome village buildings date from those heady affluent days. The two-storey market house, now occupied by the National Trust, is older. Something of the spirit of the Wild West attaches to the boom times of lead mining: self-administered law protecting rights and claims, miners' camps, and mines with names such as 'Good Luck', 'Leather Ears', 'Tear Breeches', 'Hopping Pipe', 'Haveadventur', and, 'Brandy Bottle'.

The Miners' Standard, named after the lead miners' 14-pint standard bronze measuring dish that had to be filled with ore of sufficient quality for a mine to be approved, pre-dates the burst of growth, dating from 1633. It has a distinctive pick and shovel sign and stands at the southern edge of the village where it once served Islington, a long vanished shantytown community of workers attracted by jobs in the mines. In an excellent sales pitch beer was promoted as an antidote to lead poisoning. The toxicity of lead was a problem for livestock as well as people. Cattle and sheep exposed to high concentrations of residues on land near workings were liable to develop a fatal disease known as 'the belland'. Animals, however, were not encouraged to prop up the bar for a protective pint or two.

South of Winster, beside the line of an old track in fields near Shothouse Spring, is a packhorse trail guidepost. These stone waymarkers began to be set up in the early years of the 18th century. A few survive and can be discovered beside old trails although some have been re-erected away from their original location. On the four faces of this post 'Matlock', 'Ashborn', 'Bakewel' and 'Chesterfeild' can be clearly made out. A further inscription has been added; dated 1757 it announces, 'Near this place lies ...' but the rest has weathered away. Presumably some individual deemed unworthy of a place in the consecrated ground of a churchyard lies buried near this isolated spot.

❧ WIRKSWORTH

There are those things that are physically hidden. Concealed from sight. Others are hidden in the past, lost behind the veil of time. Yet others are obscured by lack of comprehension. Language can guard secrets and in common with many close-knit communities the lead miners of Derbyshire developed arcane usages impenetrable to the uninitiated. Wirksworth was one of the county's chief lead-producing towns. It still holds its Barmote Court in Chapel Lane although it is now more about maintaining tradition than real business. The court once ruled on the ancient laws and customs that protected the rights and privileges of the common man to prospect for lead and follow the seams pretty much where they liked with the exception of churchyards, orchards, gardens or under highways.

Set in the base of wall at the south transept of the church of St Mary is a small, naive carving of a lead miner. The stone was found near Bonsall and incorporated when the church was built in the 13th century. Known as 't'owd man', the phrase symbolises Wirksworth and lead mining and can be used to refer to miner, mine workings, waste, or to the ore itself. T'owd man is shown with his pick and 'kibble', the basket or 'wisket' in which ore was carried. On the hills above the town can be found the 'boles' or hearths where smelting took place before the big companies with their furnaces took over from t'owd man. Ore was crushed with a hammer called a 'bucker' then washed or 'buddled' to separate the heavier lead-bearing rock. After buddling it was sieved in a 'jig' before being placed in the 'bole'. A bole was usually nothing more than a simple hollow surrounded by stones. Ore and wood were loaded in layers for firing. Exposed sites were chosen making maximum use of any prevailing wind to supplement the air pumped from manual bellows and help raise the temperature in the hearth sufficiently to smelt the lead to the point where the molten metal could be run off into a crucible.

As you stroll around the winding streets of Wirksworth, and particularly if you visit the fascinating confusion of lanes near Dale End, sometimes called 'The Puzzle Gardens', think about the maze of diggings below ground here where t'owd man once pursued the veins of precious ore.

YEAVELEY

—— Yeaveley is well off the beaten track. Even more isolated, a mile or so west of the village along a rutted track, is Stydd Hall. A sturdy four-square farmhouse, mostly Elizabethan, but with earlier foundations, traces of a square moat and later additions. In the garden, one ruined wall of a 13th century chapel with the arches of three windows intact can be seen. This is all that remains of a preceptory that belonged to the Knights Hospitallers (see also Barrow upon Trent entry) who had been made a gift of land here by Richard I. From its beginnings as a community of brothers caring for pilgrims and crusaders in the Holy Land, the order developed into a military one. Knights were recruited from the noble families of the land and preceptories acted as a kind of enrolment and induction centre.

❦ YOULGREAVE

— Youlgreave has an interesting collection of houses, big and small. Thimble Hall is one up, one down and each room only 8 feet square. Youlgreave Hall and the Old Hall are both said to be 17th century, though the latter by its name and appearance one may assume to be earlier. Most of the village is stretched out along its main road and few people look beyond but there is much to discover. Behind Old Hall is a fine example of a typical Derbyshire manor farmhouse with a hall and crosswings, mullioned windows and roof of stone slates. A series of steep and narrow stone-flagged pedestrian alleys, some equipped with street lighting, wind down between houses clinging to the dale side. At the foot of Holywell Lane a clapper bridge of indeterminate age crosses the river Bradford. Built from stone slabs laid on piers, clapper bridges are a simple but effective design. Such bridges were once thought to be Bronze Age but could in fact date from any time from prehistory to the Middle Ages.

INDEX